Artificial Intelligence and Machine Learning for Business

A No-Nonsense Guide to Data Driven Technologies

Third Edition

Steven Finlay

Relativistic

Relativistic

e-mail: AI@relativistic.co.uk

ISBN-13: 978-1-999-73034-5

ISBN-10: 1-999-73034-8

No plants or animals were mistreated in the writing of this book.

Cover image: "Fire in the blood." Thanks to Pixabay.

To Sam and Ruby

Contents

Acknowledgements

I would like to thank my family, and my wife Samantha in particular, for their support in writing this book. I would also like to extend my gratitude to all those readers of the previous edition who contacted me with suggestions, corrections, thoughts and ideas. I have incorporated the majority of these into this edition. I am particularly grateful to the reader who told me where I could buy an orange washing machine.

Foreword

56 minutes one way. 112 minutes for the round trip. That's the time it takes my commuter train to travel from my home town of Preston to the great British city of Manchester and back. I find this is an ideal time to catch up on a bit of reading. Therefore, I thought that a concise book about artificial intelligence and machine learning, which could be read in about this time, would be useful to people with not much free time on their hands.

An understanding of machine learning is important because it's having a huge impact across many aspects of our lives. In particular, it's driving the explosion in "Artificial intelligence" applications in many areas such as language translation, autonomous robots and medical diagnosis.

Artificial intelligence and machine learning are also having a direct impact on many everyday business functions. Automated systems, based on machine learning, are replacing numerous tasks that were once undertaken by people. This is giving organizations which embrace these technologies a competitive advantage over their rivals because of the efficiency savings and improved customer service that such systems can deliver.

This new and updated edition of the book is considerably longer than the previous one. In particular, there are several new chapters covering a broader set of topics than before. However, I have striven to retain the "concise no-nonsense" style of the original. Not least, because this was a key feature that readers said they liked about it. Therefore, the book may now take a little longer than 112 minutes to read (maybe two round trips to Manchester rather than one), but I hope you find the time well spent.

1. Introduction

Do you have a smartphone or a credit card? Do you buy stuff from supermarkets or play computer games? Are you employed or use health care? If the answer to any of these questions is yes, then artificial intelligence and machine learning will be having an impact on your life in one way or another. This is because they are the primary tools organizations use to leverage the data they hold about you in order to decide how they are going to deal with you. They are used to inform organizations about how you are likely to behave under different circumstances, and hence the way that they should treat you in order to maximize their (and sometimes your) objectives.

These technologies are now being used in almost every walk of life to improve processes and enhance peoples' everyday experiences via "artificially intelligent" machines and computer interfaces. Amazon's Echo, Apple's Siri and Google Translate are just three well known software products that demonstrate the benefits that these technologies can deliver.

These days, many products and services are also adaptive. They tailor their responses to the behavior of individual users. TV and music streaming services learn to identify the content you like, and present you with recommendations that you'll no doubt be interested in. Change the type of music you listen to and their recommendations will change too. Likewise, you can buy heating systems which learn to anticipate when it's the best time to turn the heating on so that you don't have to bother, while at the same time optimizing energy usage to reduce your bills. These are further examples of artificial intelligence in action.

This concise text provides a managerial (i.e. non-technical and no complex formulas) overview of artificial intelligence and machine learning, what they are and how they are used. No prior knowledge is assumed. To put it another way, if you can read and write and do basic arithmetic (there is a bit of arithmetic, but not that much) then you should be OK with the material in this book.

A good question to ask at this point is: why do I need to know about these things? One reason is personal. Intelligent decision-making systems, based on machine learning, are widely used by organizations to decide how to treat you, your friends and your family. They use these tools to decide if you will receive a great offer or a poor one, if you should be placed at the front or the back of the queue, if you will be subject to a tax audit or treated as a suspect in a criminal case. Therefore, it's not a bad idea to know something about these things so that you can understand why an organization may have treated you in one way and not in another.

The other reason to learn about artificial intelligence, and the one that is the main focus of this book, is that it is now a mainstream business tool. Not that long ago, artificial intelligence was the domain of a few nerdy specialists working mainly in academia, financial services or large marketing departments. These days, regardless of what business you are in, applications of artificial intelligence, based on machine learning, can be found across the full range of business activities. This covers everything from employee vetting, answering customer queries and target marketing through to robots on the production line, warehouse management and customer deliveries. As a consequence, artificial intelligence is supporting or supplanting human expertise in many domains. Some examples include: replacing underwriters when setting insurance premiums, helping HR professionals decide who to hire/fire, automatically identifying customers as they walk into your store and supporting doctors when diagnosing illnesses such as cancer and heart disease.

Artificial intelligence has arrived big time. It's no fad and it's here to stay. Those organizations which can use it to solve business problems, improve efficiency and cut costs will benefit at the expense of their rivals.

This doesn't mean that you need to learn all the things that a technical specialist (a data scientist) needs to know. However, having a working knowledge of what artificial intelligence and machine learning are, and knowing how they can be used to help your organization deliver better products and services, will be beneficial. Not least, because in order to make effective use of these tools they need to be focused on business objectives to address specific problems that organizations face.

If on the other hand you happen to be an equation quoting, formula juggling, bad ass mathematical genius who thinks they know all there is to know about artificial intelligence, then this book may also have some value for you too. Possibly even more than those who know nothing at all. Why? Because if all you care about are the theoretical aspects of the subject then you face a real risk of hitting a brick wall when it comes to delivering useful solutions in the minefield that is the real world; a world populated with social, ethical and political issues. This, together with a growing raft of privacy and data protection legislation, could derail your solutions no matter how good they are mathematically. Without consideration of these "soft issues" the best case is that the solutions you develop don't get to be deployed. The worst-case scenario is that you design an artificial intelligence based system that lands you in court because it unfairly discriminates against minorities, women or some other group of people. Maybe you can skip a few of the earlier chapters, but you should certainly read the later ones.

To get the most out of artificial intelligence, data scientists need to engage with business users to understand their problems. Data scientists also need to understand an organization's culture and its approach to the adoption of new ideas, technologies and working practices. Legal and regulatory issues in the region(s) in which their clients operate also require due consideration. It doesn't matter how good a solution is in terms of cutting edge hardware and software, if it's not aligned with an organization's business objectives and operational processes, then it's all just a waste of time and money.

Lots of solution suppliers can bamboozle you with their fancy tech and the latest terminology, which is often just a rebranding of last year's tech with a new twist. However, the suppliers who add value will be those who spend time understanding how you and your organization work. They will then determine if and how their solutions can be used to improve what you do and explain this to you in simple language which you can understand without needing to reach for Wikipedia.

Successful artificial intelligence is a two-way thing. Data scientists need to know something about your organization and what it does, and you need to understand a little bit about artificial intelligence and machine learning. Without this joint understanding it's unlikely that you or your organization will be able to realize the full benefits that artificial intelligence has to offer.

OK. So, what will you learn from reading this book? The key topics that we are going to cover in the following chapters are:

- What machine learning and artificial intelligence are.

- The sort of things organizations use artificial intelligence for.

- What a predictive model looks like.

- The relationship between artificial intelligence, machine learning and "Big Data."

- The people and tools needed to apply artificial intelligence.

- How to use artificial intelligence to improve business processes and the bottom line.

- The legal and ethical issues that need to be considered when developing artificial intelligence based solutions that are going to be used to make decisions about people.

- How advanced forms of machine learning are applied to drive artificial intelligence applications such as object recognition and language translation.

- The current limitations of machine learning and artificial intelligence.

Recommended further reading and a glossary of common machine learning/artificial intelligence terms are provided in Appendices B and C respectively.

2. What are Machine Learning and Artificial Intelligence (AI)?

Machine learning is the use of mathematical procedures (**algorithms**) to analyze data. The aim is to discover useful patterns (relationships or correlations) between different items of data. Once the relationships have been identified, these can be used to make inferences about the behavior of new cases when they present themselves. In essence, this is analogous to the way people learn. We observe what goes on around us and draw conclusions from our experiences about how the world works. We then apply what we have learnt to help us deal with new situations that we find ourselves in. The more we experience and learn, the better our ability to make decisions becomes.

One application of machine learning is object recognition. The goal is to develop systems that can identify everyday objects from images the system is presented with. The data used to develop an object recognition system consists of pictures of different objects such as chairs, umbrellas, washing machines and so on. Each picture presented to the machine learning algorithm is labeled to identify which type of object it contains. For each type of object there may be hundreds or thousands of different images, representing alternative forms of that object from different perspectives (you'd be surprised at just how many variants of an umbrella there are!)

By analyzing the different images, machine learning algorithms recognize that certain objects are associated with certain features (patterns). Chairs tend to have protuberances (legs) coming from a flat, often squarish base (the seat). They are also differentiated from stools by having a back rest. Washing machines tend to be cube shaped with knobs on and are almost never pink or orange (please, do let me know if you ever come across somewhere where I can buy a pink washing machine!) Similarly, umbrellas are long and thin (when closed), are often, but not always, black and so on.

One of the most common, and arguably the first, application of machine learning is prediction. It's about using machine learning to determine something that you don't currently know, based on the information that you currently have available. The patterns that one finds relate to the relationships between behaviors and outcomes. Very often this relates to people's past behavior and what they subsequently went on to do. Having identified the relationships that exist, it is then possible to make predictions about someone's future behavior based on their current state of being. If you give me a sample of peoples' previous purchasing history, I can utilize machine learning to identify patterns in their purchase behavior. I can then use these patterns to predict what goods someone is likely to buy next; i.e. future purchases are the outcome that I want to predict. This allows me to target them with tailored promotional offers for those specific products.

Using machine learning for prediction is sometimes referred to as predictive modelling or **Predictive Analytics** (PA). In fact, predictive analytics is such a common application of machine learning that many people (rightly or wrongly) often use the two terms interchangeably.

Predicting the future behavior of individuals is what people usually associate with machine learning, but there are other situations and problems to which machine learning can be applied. All you need is some unknown event or thing that you want to determine (predict), and this could be in the past, present or future. Doctors examine their patients, carry out tests and question them about their symptoms in order to gather evidence (data). They then use this data to come to a view as to what they think is wrong with the patient. They are not making a prediction about the patient's future health but trying to work out what's wrong with them today. Doctors can do this with a high degree of accuracy because they cross reference the patient information that they have obtained against what they have learnt from years of training and practice. In other words, they are looking for how the patient's symptoms correlate with their knowledge of known illnesses. Machine learning can be applied in the same way. Given a host of detailed information about the symptoms of different illnesses, machine learning can be used to estimate the probability that someone has a certain condition, based on the symptoms that they present.

Another way to think about machine learning/predictive analytics is as a method of reducing uncertainty. There are a whole host of possible outcomes that could occur in any given situation. Machine learning won't tell you with absolute certainty which outcome will occur, but it can provide some insight into the likelihood, or odds, of each outcome.

You may know that when someone goes grocery shopping they often buy bread, wine and chicken, but with machine learning you can determine that there is say, an 80% chance that the next product they buy is bread, a 15% chance that they buy wine and a 5% chance that they buy chicken. Therefore, if you want to encourage them to make their next purchase in your store, you are far more likely to win their custom with a bread offer rather than a wine or chicken offer.

A **predictive model** (or just model going forward) is the output generated by the machine learning process. The model captures the relationships (patterns) that have been uncovered by the analytics process. Once a model has been created, it can be used to generate new predictions. Organizations then use the model's predictions to decide what to do or how to treat people. So, machine learning is a process and a predictive model is the end product of that process.

There are lots of different types of predictive model, and there are dozens, if not hundreds, of machine learning techniques and algorithms that can be used to generate a model. However, regardless of the type of model or the mathematics used to create it, a model's predictions are almost always represented by a number - a **score**. The higher the score the more likely someone is to behave in the way the model predicts, the lower the score the less likely they are to behave in that way.

Machine learning can be applied in all sorts of situations and to many types of problem. However, the most common business applications of machine learning, and the ones that are the main focus of this book, relate to what people are going to do or how they will behave in the future, based on what you know about them today[1].

One very well-known application of machine learning is credit scoring. When someone wants a loan, credit card or mortgage the lender asks the individual questions about themselves and their lifestyle. They then combine this with information from a credit report containing details about the individual's previous borrowing history, provided by a credit reference agency such as Experian or Equifax[2]. The information is then fed into a predictive model to generate a credit score.

If you live in the USA you will probably be familiar with FICO and/or Vantage scores. A high score (>750) is a prediction that someone is very likely to repay any money they borrow; i.e. that they are creditworthy. A low score (<500) indicates that someone is very uncreditworthy. Banks and finance companies the world over use similar credit scoring methods.

Another common application of machine learning is target marketing. Given information about someone's age, gender, income, web-browsing, purchase history, location and so on, a marketing department can predict if the person is interested in a particular product or not. They then use that prediction to decide whether or not to target them with promotional offers. Likewise, predictive models can also be used to infer how much people are willing to pay for products like insurance. This information is then used to tailor a personalized pricing strategy to each person's individual circumstances.

A further example of machine learning in action is preventative health care. Traditional health care systems are reactive. People seek medical assistance when they feel ill. Doctors then do their best to treat the illnesses they are presented with – treatments that can be very costly and time consuming. These days, advanced health care systems are increasingly focusing their attention on prevention rather than cure. This vastly reduces costs and improves patient outcomes. Machine learning is used to assess people's medical records and predict the likelihood of them developing specific conditions such as heart disease or diabetes, often years in advance. Individuals who come at the top of the pile; i.e. those that the model predicts are most likely to get the disease, are contacted with a view of initiating preventative action. For example, making lifestyle changes or taking preventative medication.

A final example of machine learning in action is determining what type of news (and other) articles to recommend to people. Social media providers use machine learning to analyze what articles you've read in the past and the type of topics you discuss with friends. This then drives the content that they promote to you.

That's just a few ways in which machine learning is being used. Today, machine learning supports a huge range of applications. In fact, almost any aspect of life that involves decision-making in one form or another. The algorithms that match people on dating sites, the technology used to detect credit card fraud and systems for identifying terrorist suspects all utilize predictive models derived using machine learning. If you want a more comprehensive list of applications then see the book by Eric Siegel[3], which details more than 120 different applications of predictive models in use today – and that's not a comprehensive list!

That brings us on to the question as to what one means by **Artificial Intelligence** or AI. There are many and varied definitions of what AI is, and as with predictive analytics, many people use the terms AI and machine learning interchangeably. In terms of the overall scope of AI research, machine learning is a key field of study, but there are many others. True artificial intelligence is about much much more than just pattern recognition and prediction. Some experts also question if true AI can ever be achieved by just following a "Brute force" approach of developing ever more complex algorithms using ever more powerful computer hardware. Is there some additional (as yet unknown) element required for human-like intelligence and self-awareness which can't be replicated via computation alone[4]?

So, in one sense it's incorrect to say that machine learning and artificial intelligence are the same thing. However, in practice almost every AI system in use today relies heavily on machine learning. Therefore, for the purposes of this book a simple working definition of AI that we shall adhere to is:

- **Artificial Intelligence (AI) is the replication of human analytical and/or decision-making capabilities.**

A good AI application is one that can perform as well or better than the average person when faced with everyday tasks. For example, the ability to identify people from their Facebook photos, being able to assess someone's creditworthiness more accurately than an experienced underwriter, the ability to beat the best Go and chess players or being better able to spot the signs of cancer on a medical scan than an expert radiologist.

At one level, AI applications can seem almost magical to the layperson. However, like most things, once you get under the bonnet the mystique evaporates. In practice, all of the news stories one hears about the amazing applications of "AI" are really just very sophisticated applications of machine leaning.

A key mistake to avoid is thinking that current AI applications are in any way intelligent in a human conscious way. Sure, they are very complex, exceedingly clever and can be creepily lifelike at times, but it's all just math at the end of the day. Most experts agree, we are years away from being able to create a machine with a human-like sense of self, or which could pass itself off as human day in, day out. That's not to say there aren't some very good chatbots out there!

All of the AI applications in use today are what the industry refers to as **Narrow AI**. They are very good at behaving intelligently when applied to one well defined area of expertise. However, these systems are miles away from **General AI**. General AI is a system that can learn and act intelligently across a wide range of environments and problems in a similar way to a person. An AI application that is used to detect tax avoidance for example, is useless at detecting the signs of cancer from medical scans. However, a person could learn to do both these tasks if they were given suitable training. In a similar vein, a system such as Google Translate is great at understanding the spoken word but wouldn't be much use when it comes to assessing if someone on a dating site might be compatible with you.

The core components that drive most AI/machine learning applications are:

- **Data input.** This can be sensory inputs from cameras (eyes), microphones (ears) or other sources. It also includes pre-processed data such as the information captured when someone fills in a form online, details of what someone has bought using their credit card or an individual's credit history provided by a credit reference agency.

- **Data (pre)processing.** The raw data input needs to be processed into a standard "computer friendly" format before it is ready to be used.

- **Predictive models.** These are generated by the machine learning process using past experiences; i.e. large amounts of historic data. Pre-processed data for new cases is fed into the models in order to generate fresh predictions going forward.

- **Decision rules (rule sets**). A prediction on its own is useless. You have to decide how to use it. Decision rules are used in conjunction with data inputs and the scores from predictive models to decide what to do. Sometimes these rules are derived automatically by the machine learning algorithm, but often they will include additional rules defined by human experts/business users.

- **Response/output.** Action needs to be taken based upon the decision(s) that have been made. If the decision is that someone is creditworthy, then a credit card needs to be issued. If the decision is that someone should be hired, then they need to be sent an offer letter, given a contract to sign and so on.

It's the combination of these individual components that give us the "AI."

What makes some AI applications appear so clever is the sheer complexity of the algorithms that underpin them, combined with a slick user interface to gather data and deliver the required responses in a human friendly way. Combine these components with the latest generation of industrial machinery, or integrate them into cars and other vehicles, and one has robots that can interact with their environment and engage with us in a very human like way.

Let's begin by considering a marketing AI application for a drinks company. The application takes information gathered about individuals from social networks and feeds it into a predictive model to determine how likely they are to buy a particular brand of whisky. The system then applies a number of rules to decide if an individual should be marketed to. The rules that might exist are:

1. If the predictive model estimates that the chance of them buying whisky is more than 90% then do nothing. They will probably buy the whisky anyway.

2. If the predictive model estimates that the chance of them buying whisky is between 1% and 90% then send them a $5 discount coupon to try and make the whisky a more attractive offering; i.e. influence the customer's behavior to increase the chance of them buying.

3. If the predictive model estimates the chance of them buying whisky to be less than 1% then don't do anything. They probably won't buy the whisky whatever you offer them. Therefore, it's not worth the effort trying to persuade them.

So, these rules would be derived based on some type of cost-benefit analysis, where the 1% and 90% cut-offs are deemed to be the optimal level at which to trigger marketing activity. However, other business rules would also come into play, such as:

1. NEVER make an offer to sell whisky to children, no matter what their propensity to buy it!

2. DO NOT send offers to people with a history of alcohol dependency.

Both groups referred to by these rules will contain lots of people who would like to buy whisky; i.e. >1% chance, but from an ethical perspective targeting children or people with alcohol problems is difficult to argue for. From a purely profit-orientated perspective, marketing to children is likely to be illegal and targeting such individuals could result in a significant amount of negative publicity. These two rules are a great example of why human expertise is required to support automated machine learning based systems, especially where systems are being used to make risky or controversial decisions about people.

One highly publicized example of the algorithms running wild is the case of YouTube and its ad placement policy. In 2017, many large organizations withdrew their advertising from YouTube. This was because YouTube were found to be placing some of their adverts alongside material from terrorists and other unsavory sources. It was YouTube's machine learning algorithms which decided which ads to place where that had caused the problem. Consequently, YouTube had to undertake a major review of its ad placement process[5]. As a result, many months later in 2018, they decided to revert to a manual vetting process. Every video clip had to be reviewed and approved by a real person before it was included in YouTube's service which paired advertisers with popular content[6].

A reasonable question to ask is why it took almost a year for YouTube to figure out a solution? One can't be certain as to the reason, but a very plausible answer is that they spent a lot of time trying to solve the problem using a solely automated (machine learning/AI) approach, before realizing that they needed to maintain a human element in the assessment process.

The final thing required from an AI system is to issue the required response. In the whisky example, this is to send an appropriate discount code or coupon to the individuals who have been targeted. What this means is that in order to deliver the required action, the AI application needs to be linked to the organization's marketing channels. If the AI is telling you that the appropriate response is to text millions of customers with offers, then it needs to be connected to the systems that can send texts. If texts, coupons, internet pop-ups, or whatever are being used to communicate the offers, then there is still a need for someone to design the wording and format of the communications in a way that is both appealing to customers and complies with relevant marketing legislation.

The vast majority of AI applications rely heavily on prediction, driven by pattern recognition (i.e. machine learning/predictive analytics). Take speech recognition systems that support tools such as Apple's Siri and Amazon's Echo. Upon hearing a sound, a speech recognition system pre-processes that sound into a number of standardized soundbites. It will then try to identify what word it thinks has been spoken. This is based on a set of probabilities (scores) generated by a predictive model created using machine learning. If the system calculates that there is a 5% chance that the sound is "Hello" 20% that it's "Jell-O" and 75% that it's "Mellow" then it will make an educated guess that the word spoken was "Mellow."

Advanced AI systems use layers of complex predictive models in combination to formulate a view as to what is going on around them, given the inputs that they receive. The next layer of the speech recognition system will consider phrases and word structure. The predictive elements of the system are then combined with decision rules (decision logic) to determine what actions to take when certain words or phrases are spoken.

One common misconception is that machine learning and artificial intelligence are completely new, only entering the mainstream in the last few years. The reality is that research into business applications of machine learning was first undertaken in the early 1940s[7] and machine learning has been used in the financial services industry since the 1950's (credit scoring). Machine learning techniques were then applied to areas such as direct marketing, tax collection and insurance underwriting not long after that. Recent developments have been to put these types of tool into the home, into smartphones and other devices.

Some machine learning/AI experts might dispute this view of

history, arguing that it's only with recent technological advances that machine learning has come into its own. However, if your definition of machine learning/AI encompasses using algorithms to identify patterns of behavior which drive autonomous decision-making systems, and these systems significantly outperform human experts, then the credit scoring systems of the 1950s satisfy that definition.

What has changed in recent times are three things. First is the terminology. In the 1980s/1990s what is now termed machine learning/AI came under the title of "Data Mining" or "computational statistics." It's also the case that the theory underpinning the most common machine learning approaches in use today were developed before or during the 1990s[8] (although many have been refined and extended since then).

The second thing that has changed is the computer hardware and software that underpin machine learning. The shift to placing services online via smartphones, tablets and the internet means that there is now so much more information available about people than ever before, and the amount of information continues to grow year on year. The speed and storage capabilities of computers has also increased considerably. This makes it possible to process huge amounts of data quickly and cost effectively. Likewise, the complexity of machine learning algorithms and the predictive models they generate has increased by many orders of magnitude in just a few years.

In parallel with the advances in hardware and algorithm design, there are now a whole host of software tools available for machine learning. Much of it free and/or open source (such as the R and Python programming languages) and available via one's PC, laptop or cloud services offered by the IT giants such as Microsoft[9] and Google[10].

The third thing which has changed is the way that we interact with the underlying models and decision rules. We no longer have to type very rigid instructions on keyboards or have to interpret pages of detailed mathematical output. Instead, modern AI systems interact with us in much more human-like ways.

Often the interfaces between humans and computers are themselves based on machine learning principles, driven by predictive models. If we return to the whisky sales example, I could use machine learning in the design of a chatbot to talk to people on social media about their drinking habits. The data gathered by the chatbot then supplements other data that I've gathered about people. If the whisky application determines that people should be given a discount offer, then this could be relayed back to customers via the chatbot in a conversational form, rather than the more traditional approach of sending them a coupon or discount code via text or e-mail.

The same principle applies to digital personal assistants such as Amazon's Echo. One set of algorithms are used to translate what you say into soundbites (data pre-processing). The pre-processed soundbites are then fed into another set of predictive models which try to predict what outcome you are asking for; such as playing a certain song or asking about the weather. Amazon allows developers to use this pre-processing capability for free[11] – allowing anyone to incorporate advanced speech recognition into their programs and apps.

What all this means is that the cost of entry into the world of machine learning and AI has reduced considerably. Only a few years ago machine learning was primarily the domain of large businesses and academic institutions. Today, anyone with a laptop and some time on their hands can get involved and start building predictive models relatively quickly and at almost zero cost, and then develop an advanced user interface to implement those models as an "AI app."

These days, there are even competition websites for machine learning such as Kaggle[12]. Organizations provide their data for free, and then amateur and professional teams compete to see who can build the model with the greatest predictive power using the data that has been provided. The winner shares their approach with the organization that supplied that data and receives a prize in return. The rewards for winning a Kaggle competition are significant. Typical cash prizes are a few thousand dollars, but the largest prizes are in excess of a million![13] However, for many winners, the prize money is only a secondary consideration to the high salaries that Kaggle winners can command.

When discussing machine learning, predictive modelling and AI you will probably also come across the terms **data science** and **data scientist**. Data science isn't a science in the same way that physics, chemistry or biology are. It's simply a description of the application of machine learning techniques. Likewise, a data scientist is someone who can apply machine learning in a practical way. It's about more than just the mathematical aspects of the subject. A good data scientist also has an understanding of data and IT systems and is able to understand the business context in which their solutions will be applied.

3. What Do the Scores Generated by a Predictive Model Represent?

As noted in the previous chapter, the vast majority of machine learning/AI applications used in business rely on predictive models. These models generate numbers (scores) which indicate what is likely to occur, based on the information that the model is presented with.

The scores generated by a predictive model can be one of two types:

1. **Probability (likelihood) scores.** These predict the likelihood of specific events. For example, will someone do something or not? The technical name for a predictive model of this type is a **classification model.**

2. **Magnitude (quantity) scores.** These predict the amount or size of something. For example, how much someone is going to spend in store, or how long before they do something. The technical name for a predictive model of this type is a **regression model.**

Classification models predict the likelihood that events occur. Often these events will be binary in nature; i.e. a single score is generated, representing the likelihood that the event will occur. However, classification models can also be used to address problems with multiple outcomes (events).

Common business applications of classification models include:

- **Medical diagnosis.** The score is a measure of the likelihood of someone having or getting a particular illness.

- **Content detection.** The model predicts if media content relates to a certain subject/topic. Models of this type are used by social media companies to identify offensive or illegal material posted to their sites. High scoring material is blocked or placed in a queue for review by a human assessor.

- **Customer attrition.** The model generates a probability that a customer will buy rival products or stop using a product or service. For example, switching their utility provider, acquiring a new credit card or cancelling a magazine subscription.

- **Fraud detection.** The score generated by the model represents the probability that a fraudulent transaction is occurring. For example, someone trying to buy something with a stolen credit card.

- **Dating compatibility.** The model score provides an indication of how likely two people are to hit it off on a date.

- **Product recommendation.** The score represents the likelihood that someone will buy a given product or service. Customers are only marketed to if the probability of them buying the product or service is sufficiently high.

- **Staff retention.** The model estimates the probability that an employee will leave their current position to take up another post.

- **Machine breakdown.** The score predicts if a machine is likely to fail in the near future. This allows for pre-emptive action such as texting a driver that they need to come to the garage to get their car fixed before it breaks down.

Sometimes the scores from a classification model represent a probability directly. A person who receives a score of 0.0 certainly won't experience the event. Those with a score of 1.0 certainly will. Predictive models don't provide perfect predictions. What one tends to see is a spread (a distribution) of probabilities between 0.0 and 1.0 for individuals within the population. When a product recommendation model generates a score of 0.70 for someone, this means that the model predicts that there is a 70% chance that the individual will buy the product and a 30% chance that they won't.

In other situations, the score from a classification model is transformed to a certain scale. If we return to the world of credit scoring, credit scores tend to be scaled to range from about 400 to about 800[14]. If someone receives a score of 400 it means that they are very unlikely to repay any credit advanced to them (<5% chance that the loan will be repaid). A score of 800 means that they will almost certainly repay their debt (>99.9% chance that the loan will be repaid).

Most classification models used in business generate a single score. The score predicts a simple yes/no type event, such as those described in the aforementioned list. Where machine learning is applied to problems with multiple outcomes, then a separate score is produced for each possible outcome.

Taken to their extreme, some of the most advanced predictive models in use today generate thousands of scores. Each score represents the probability of one possible outcome. An object recognition system, designed to identify everyday objects in pictures, is one such example. The system generates a score (probability) for each object it's been trained to identify. Score 1 predicts a 4% chance it's a picture of a washing machine, Score 2 a 6% chance it's an umbrella, Score 3 an 80% chance it's a chair and so on. The score associated with "Chair" is the highest and therefore the system would "Guess" that the object is a chair.

For complex applications such as object and speech recognition, business users won't see the scores generated directly. Instead, an overarching set of decision rules will be applied to translate the scores into something more meaningful, with the results delivered via a suitable "customer friendly" interface.

Regression models on the other hand are all about quantities; i.e. the magnitude of an event. Some examples of business applications of regression models are:

- **Life expectancy.** The score provides a prediction as to how long a person is expected to live. This type of model is often used to set life insurance premiums and pension annuities.

- **Journey time.** Given information about your driving habits, current location and driving conditions, when are you likely to arrive at your destination?

- **Credit loss.** When someone defaults on a loan, how much of the debt is likely to be written-off?

- **Spend.** The model score predicts how much someone is likely to spend in their local supermarket in the next 12 months.

- **Purchase interval.** How long after buying a product can a repeat purchase be expected? Marketing activity can then be timed to occur shortly before the customer is expected to buy the product again.

- **Call length.** How long is a phone call predicted to last? This aids with resource planning in call centres.

- **Occupancy.** Predicting what time of day someone is likely to be at home and hence the best time to visit them.

- **Response time.** How long after an action is taken is a response observed? After sending someone a letter, e-mail or text, how long does it take for them to reply?

In some cases, the score from a regression model is a direct estimate of what one is trying to predict. A spend model that generates a score of 5,981 means that the customer is predicted to spend $5,981. In other situations, the score is scaled to represent percentiles or to allocate a grade from 1 to 10, A to E, or similar. Grade A represents the very best (most profitable) customers, Grade E the least profitable ones.

Both regression and classification models are widely used, but classification models tend to be the most popular, particularly for common business applications. This is because simple will they/won't they type events have traditionally been the easiest for organizations to understand. There also tends to be less ambiguity in how problems are defined. This makes it simpler for data scientists to translate business objectives into an appropriate numerical representation that the machine learning process can be applied to. Defining if a customer buys whisky or not is pretty straight forward (classification). However, determining the profitability of an individual whisky sale is far more complex (regression).

What type of model to use (regression or classification) depends very much on what one wants to do with the model scores. If all I'm interested in is identifying which credit card customers are most likely to move to a competitor, then what I need is a classification model to predict the probability of attrition. A retention strategy (such as offering a discount or free gift) is then applied to try to retain those customers most likely to defect.

If on the other hand, my primary concern is to identify profitable customers with the aim of encouraging them to spend more, then what I need is a regression model. The model is designed to predict who are going to be the big spenders and target those. I don't need to bother with the rest of the customer base.

There is however, a third option. Let's say that what I'm really interested in doing is retaining profitable customers, and I don't care about losing the unprofitable ones who don't spend much on their cards. In this situation, then possibly the best approach is to build two separate predictive models as follows:

1. An attrition model to predict those customers most likely to defect to a rival product (Classification).

2. A revenue model to identify which customers spend the most (Regression).

The two models are then used in combination to drive a retention strategy as shown in Figure 1.

Figure 1. Using two models in combination.

		Probability of defecting to rival product (Score from attrition model)		
		Low	Medium	High
Estimated spend (Score from revenue model)	Low	Do nothing	Do nothing	Do nothing
	Medium	Do nothing	Do nothing	Apply retention strategy 1
	High	Do nothing	Apply retention strategy 1	Apply retention strategy 2

Figure 1 uses the scores from each model to segment the population by both revenue and attrition. By using the two models in combination, a tailored set of retention strategies can be applied and significant cost savings achieved. This is because resources aren't spent trying to retain customers that won't attrite or those that have a high probability of attrition, but who don't spend much on their cards.

For the example in Figure 1, three differential strategies are applied:

1. Do nothing for the "worst" customers. It is not cost effective to try and retain these.

2. Undertake a light touch (i.e. low cost) retention strategy for those in the middle (strategy 1).

3. Expend the most effort on the "best" group of customers (strategy 2).

Of course, there are alternative formulations of this problem. One could build a single predictive model that only tries to predict the very highest revenue generating customers who are also likely to attrite, and these are then targeted. This is certainly a reasonable approach, but it would result in a loss of granularity about the nature of customers; i.e. a single model would not allow you to explore the trade-off between attrition and revenue which the twin model approach, as illustrated in Figure 1, provides.

Note that the models only provide predictions about what customers will do. They don't tell you what should then be done on the basis of those predictions. With regards to what activities should be undertaken for retention strategies 1 and 2, that's an additional consideration that the organization needs to address within the overall scope of its machine learning project. This is important because quite a common failing is for organizations to build some very good predictive models, and then not use them for anything. Making the right decisions and then acting upon those decisions is vital if a machine learning project is going to be successful.

4. Why Use Machine Learning? What Value Does it Add?

Applications of machine learning, based on predictive models, are increasingly being used to replace and/or supplement expert judgement and manual decision-making in all sorts of areas. This is because predictive models tend to be:

- **More accurate than human experts.** Predictive models sometimes get their predictions wrong just like people, but the overwhelming evidence is that on average they don't get it wrong quite as often. In many fields, predictive models consistently outperform human experts by 20-30%; i.e. they make 20-30% fewer errors or identify 20-30% better (more important/more profitable) cases.

- **Unbiased.** Unlike people, predictive models don't display deliberate *prejudicial* bias against someone because of their gender, race, disability, etc. Don't get me wrong, predictive models do display bias, but if designed correctly they will only give certain individuals or groups higher or lower scores than the population at large if this is based on hard statistical evidence – it's not based on some unfounded preconception or stereotype.

- **Fast**. As part of an automated decision-making system, a predictive model can be used to predict the behavior of millions of individuals in seconds. In most cases, it would be unfeasibly expensive and time consuming to have people manually making the same judgements.

- **Cheap**. Once developed, predictive models are often cheaper to deploy than their human counterparts. Although one must not forget the upfront cost associated with the initial development, plus ongoing maintenance and licensing costs.

In summary, predictive models can be used to make better, cheaper and faster decisions than those made by human experts. What this means is that in many areas predictive models are replacing people. In particular, white collar roles that require highly trained staff to use their expert judgement to decide what to do.

This is a phenomenon that began in the USA back in the 1950s and 1960s in financial services. This was a time when most applications for mortgages, automobile credit and personal loans were assessed by human underwriters who individually reviewed each loan application. They then came to a decision as to whether or not that person was creditworthy, and should therefore, get the credit that they had applied for.

In large organizations, entire office buildings were taken up by underwriting teams who spent their days making lending decisions. In local bank branches, the Bank Manager was king – a respected member of the local community with absolute discretion over who could be given a loan or mortgage and who could not. Sometimes getting a loan would simply be down to whether he (and invariably it was a he) was in a good mood that day. You were probably more likely to get a loan on a Friday afternoon, when he was feeling in a good mood about the weekend, than first thing on a Monday morning!

By the late 1980s, most of these roles were redundant. The role of bank manager had been reduced to little more than that of a salesperson – fronting the customer relationship but having no decision-making capability. The vast majority of lending decisions were being made by credit scoring models sitting at the heart of an automated decision-making system located at head office. In the world of credit granting these days, only unusual or borderline cases tend to be reviewed by a human being – the vast majority of lending decisions are made automatically without any human intervention at all.

Job losses are a concern for those in affected industries, but it's not all doom and gloom. In many cases, machine learning is adding value to roles rather than supplanting them. In hospitals and doctors' surgeries, predictive models supplement doctors' own judgements rather than replacing them. In marketing, improved targeting, based on machine learning, is used to reduce nuisance calls and junk mail, while at the same time maximizing worthwhile customer contacts; i.e. only phone/text/e-mail people who are very likely to be interested in what you are selling. In the past, blanket contact strategies were common. Staff in call centers would be supplied with phone books and told to work their way through them, calling as many people as they could regardless of their propensity to buy the product or service on offer. HR departments also make use of machine learning to pre-screen job applications to remove those least likely to be suited to a given role. This allows HR staff to concentrate more of their time on the most promising prospects.

Another opportunity that machine learning makes possible is forecasting new types of behavior that were not considered or were not cost effective before. In policing for example, predictive models are helping police officers narrow down suspect lists and better target crime, improving efficiency and giving them more time to focus on the most serious crimes. Predictive models are also fundamental to "people matching" services such as dating and job sites. Without predictive models these would be very different affairs – matching people based on a very crude set of criteria and/or having to use people to do the matching, making such services very much more expensive and less efficient.

Despite all the arguments in favor of automated decision-making systems based on predictive models, don't make the mistake of thinking that machine learning is perfect. Predictive models can and do get things wrong on a frequent basis, but on average just not quite as often as people. In a similar vein, if there are problems or biases with the data feeding the algorithms used to construct a predictive model, then the resulting models will be flawed. Also, if the people who design the decision-making system make incorrect assumptions about how a predictive model is going to be used, then again, the model won't work well. Imagine that you want to use machine learning to identify senior managers who are responsible for managing teams of people in large organizations. The purpose, once they have been identified, is to ask them to contribute to a cross-industry response to the government's new legislation for improved childcare provision. The model may be very predictive, but it will inevitably be biased toward men. Why? Because we live in a society that still displays gender bias in most industries, and a society where women are still viewed as the primary source of childcare. In one sense the model will be accurate as long as it identifies senior leaders, but there will be a resulting under-representation of women reflecting the societal biases that exist.

One real life situation that has been highly publicized is that of granting prisoners parole. It has been reported that the algorithms used to support parole decisions in the US have a very strong racial bias[15]. If you are white you are far more likely to get parole than inmates of other ethnicities. Why? Because the predictive models used to assess parole cases have been developed using information about historical decisions that were themselves biased. It all comes back to the data used in the machine learning process. If the data contains information relating to previously biased decisions, then that will certainly be picked up by any machine learning algorithm. To put it another way, machine learning has no social awareness and no conscience. If there are patterns in the data that are ethically undesirable or illegal, the machine learning process has no way of knowing that. Consequently, it won't treat these socially unacceptable patterns any differently from other patterns that it finds.

A more overt example of the bias that can be displayed by machine learning based AI systems is the chatbot Tay, which was developed by Microsoft. Tay was intended to generate automatic responses to tweets by teenagers and to adapt to new conversations as they arose. Tay ended up being withdrawn within hours because it started to tweet racist and other inappropriate content[16]. The reason that it did this was because the tweets that were being used to train it contained racist and other unacceptable material. Tay learnt these patterns and played them back in its own responses.

Tay's ability to respond using natural language could be considered almost human, but its inability to moderate its responses to cater for social and ethical norms expected by wider society was very sub-human.

Another concern is that if a data scientist has particular prejudices then it is possible for them to consciously design these into the system, subverting what the data is telling them. This however, can also work to people's benefit. If it is believed that a user does not like the decisions being made, then a well-designed system will allow the decision logic to be modified/overridden – as we discussed in relation to the whisky sale example in previous chapters.

What this means is that there needs to be oversight of machine learning based decision-making systems, and an appropriate set of checks and balances in place to ensure that the systems work in a way that is both legal and ethical. We'll talk about these issues in more detail in Chapter 13.

5. How Does Machine Learning Work?

Most machine learning applications are underpinned by predictive models. The scores generated by the model(s) then drive decision-making and the subsequent actions that are taken. So, how does a predictive model generate a score? That depends on the type of predictive model being employed, and there are quite a few options to choose from. However, the three most popular types of model, which are used in the vast majority of real world business applications, are **Scorecards** (linear models), **Decision Trees** (Classification And Regression Trees or CART) and Artificial Neural Networks (ANNs), most commonly referred to as just **Neural Networks** (NNs).

Scorecards and decision trees are relatively easy for non-technical people to understand. The model scores are calculated in a simple and transparent way. It's easy to determine why these models make the predictions that they do. Neural networks on the other hand tend to be a little more complex and "Black box" in nature. This means that it can be difficult to understand why a neural network has arrived at the score that it has, and hence why a certain decision has been made on the basis of that score. However, neural networks are an increasingly popular choice for many machine learning applications due to their propensity to deliver more accurate predictions than scorecards or decision trees in many (but not all) situations.

Advanced forms of neural networks (deep networks/deep learning) are currently at the cutting edge of machine learning/AI research. Consequently, neural networks are the models of choice for complex AI problems such as object identification, speech recognition and language translation.

To illustrate these three types of predictive model, let's return to the world of health care and focus on one specific condition: heart disease[17]. Heart disease is one of the leading causes of death worldwide. Each year, around 1 in every 1,000 of the population in western countries (UK, USA, etc.) dies from heart disease, and a significant proportion of the population live with heart conditions that may well kill them sometime down the line. If you can identify people who are highly likely to develop heart disease in the future and take preventative action to reduce that likelihood, then that will dramatically reduce human suffering and increase life expectancy. The reduction in health care costs will also be considerable.

Imagine that the government has the utopian ideal of screening everyone in the population for heart disease, with the aim of taking preventative action to reduce future incidence of the disease. One way that they could do this, is to initiate a health campaign whereby every man women and child is invited to visit their doctor. They would then have relevant investigations and diagnostics tests and be given advice on how to minimize their risk of developing heart disease in the future.

That's fine in theory, but in practice the cost of such an exercise would be immense and there would not be enough doctors available to see everyone in a realistic time. The treatment of other life-threatening conditions, such as cancer and diabetes, would be likely to suffer due to a lack of resources. In fact, the net result might actually be a reduction in the overall well-being of the population due to an over-emphasis on heart disease at the expense of other conditions.

The blanket approach of screening everyone for heart disease is clearly not realistic. However, a more achievable goal might be to aim to identify say, at least half of those that will develop heart disease in the next 5 years, yet target no more than say, 5% of the population as a whole; i.e. only 1 in 20 people are invited for the full set of tests, but the majority of those likely to get heart disease will be in that 5%. OK – so half of heart disease cases would be missed, but the cost savings make the exercise justifiable and does not threaten resources allocated to the treatment of other conditions.

To achieve this objective, we are going to need some way of identifying those most at risk. To do this, we are going to apply a machine learning approach to build a predictive model that estimates the likelihood of someone developing heart disease in the next few years (a classification model). The aim is to use the model to identify those individuals most at risk. These people will then be contacted to invite them for a check-up and lifestyle review.

The starting point for machine learning is data. Data is the fuel that feeds the analytics process. Trying to do machine learning without data is like trying to make a cake without any ingredients or washing your car without water.

To build a model of heart disease, the first task is to gather some historic patient data. For this particular problem, we are going to go back and obtain the medical records from a sample of 500,000 people (chosen at random) who didn't have any sign of heart disease five years ago. This data will include, amongst other things, things like: peoples' age, gender, their Body Mass Index (BMI)[18], blood pressure readings, previous medical history, how much they exercise, if they smoke and how much alcohol they drink. There may also be other, non-medical information available such as people's income, marital status, number of dependents, type of house they live in and so on, gathered from other sources.

This snapshot of personal data from five years ago is then matched against what happened to those people over the subsequent 5 year **forecast horizon**; i.e. a record is kept of which people went on to develop a heart condition at some time in the next 5 years and which did not. So, at this point we have two parts to the data:

- **Observation data**. This is information about people at the start of the five year period; i.e. their age, blood pressure, smoking habits and so on.

- **Outcome data**. This is a record of their health over the forecast horizon. In particular, this data records if someone developed heart disease or not.

These two types of data, when combined together, form the

development sample, which is going to be used to produce the model. Let's assume that of the 500,000 cases in the development sample, 30,000 (6%) went on to develop heart disease and the other 470,000 (94%) did not. Note that having data about people who didn't get heart disease is just as important as having data about those who did. This is because the machine learning process works by identifying differences between the two event types. A common mistake with data analysis is just to record data about the event of interest, and to forget about the "non-events." Without both event and non-event information it is very difficult to come to any meaningful conclusions using machine learning (or any other data analysis method).

The next stage of the process is where the complex mathematics comes into play. Various algorithms are applied to generate a predictive model, based on what the algorithms can infer from the data in the development sample. In particular, the algorithms seek to find relationships that correlate with events or non-events, and it is these relationships which are captured by the predictive model resulting from the machine learning process.

These days, there are lots of computer packages that will apply the relevant mathematics in order to create a model. As a rule, you don't need to be a trained data scientist to be able to generate a predictive model – the software will do it all for you.

Having said this, having some familiarity with the relevant mathematical techniques is helpful. This is because it enables you to understand the diagnostics that the software produces and to identify if there have been any issues with the model creation process. Also, there are often several parameters that need to be set within the software. An experienced data scientist will know how to tweak these parameters to generate a model that is very predictive, and which also meets any business constraints that have been imposed by the organization that commissioned it.

Often the model building process is iterative. Many test models are constructed using different algorithms before a final model is arrived at. Therefore, the analytics process needs someone who knows what they are doing to guide it so that the best overall model is arrived at.

Let's assume that the data scientist starts by considering a **scorecard** type model. For reference, the most popular algorithms for generating scorecard type models are called **Linear Regression** and **Logistic Regression**.

After using an appropriate software tool, to apply the relevant algorithm to the development sample[19], the software generates the predictive model shown in Figure 2:

Figure 2. A scorecard for predicting heart disease.

Starting score (constant)	350		
Age (years)		**Gross annual income ($)**	
<23	-57	< $22,000	11
23 - 32	-26	$22,001 - $38,000	9
33 - 41	0	$38,001 - $60,000	6
42 - 48	7	$60,001 - $94,000	0
49 - 57	15	$94,001 - $144,000	-5
58 - 64	24	>$144,000	-6
65 - 71	31		
>71	65	**Smoker ?**	
		Yes	37
BMI (weight in kg / {height in metres}^{2})		No	0
<19	2		
19 - 26	0	**Diabetic ?**	
27 - 29	8	Yes	21
30 - 32	14	No	0
>32	29		
		Cholesterol level (mg per decilitre of blood)	
Gender		Low (< 160 mg)	-2
Male	2	Normal (160 - 200 mg)	0
Female	-4	High (201 - 240 mg)	19
		Very high (>240 mg)	32
Alcohol consumption (units/week)			
0	4	**Blood pressure**	
1 - 12	0	Low (below 90/60)	3
13 - 24	5	Average (between 90/60 an	0
25 - 48	10	High (above 140/90)	36
>48	22		

Using the scorecard in Figure 2, a score for someone is calculated as follows:

- To begin, everyone is assigned the "starting score" of 350.

- All of the relevant points that apply are then added or subtracted from the starting score.

For a 45 year old female with the following characteristics:

- A BMI of 28.
- Drinks an average of 6 units of alcohol a week.
- A university graduate.
- An income of $50,000 a year.
- Smokes.
- Is not diabetic.
- Normal cholesterol levels.
- Low blood pressure.

The starting score is 350. Seven points are added due to her age, which brings the score to 357. Eight points are then added based on her BMI, four points subtracted for her gender and no points added (or subtracted) based on her alcohol consumption and so on. After adding/subtracting all of the relevant points, the final score is 404.

The individual scores in the scorecard are a representation of the patterns/relationships that the machine learning algorithm has found. For example, the increasing scores allocated to older people represent the relationship between increasing age and increasing risk of heart disease, which has been deduced from the data (the development sample) used to build the model. Likewise, smokers are allocated more points than non-smokers, representing the relationship between smoking and heart disease.

Looking at the scorecard in Figure 2, it's easy to see why scorecards are so attractive and why they are so widely used across many industry sectors. One reason is that you don't need any technical ability to see which data items contribute to the score someone receives. It's also easy to gauge the relative importance of each data item. Age contributes more points to the final score than anything else. Gender on the other hand, only makes a small contribution to the overall score. It's also the case that most data items in the model, such as smoking, alcohol consumption and blood pressure fit with what is generally known from medical studies; i.e. the relationships captured by the model look sensible and conform with what is already known about risk factors for heart disease.

The fact that the model conforms with what experts already know is useful for getting people to trust the model and be comfortable using it as a diagnostic tool in their day–to-day work. If the model gave negative points for smoking and diabetes, and positive points for normal blood pressure and being young, then that is counter to what every doctor knows. Consequently, people would not have much confidence that the model was correctly predicting the condition even if the model's predictions were correct.

This appeal to common sense is important, particularly when models are being deployed in an area for the first time. People are often suspicious of new approaches such as machine learning and may instinctively distrust something that removes the human element from the decision-making process. The more that can be done to reassure people that decisions based on the model scores are the right ones, then the easier it will be to overcome any resistance to machine learning that is encountered.

The one item in the scorecard that is perhaps slightly unexpected is the impact of someone's income. What the model is saying is that if you have a low income then you are more likely to develop heart disease. If you give this some thought, then it does make sense. If someone is on a low income they may not be able to afford gym membership (less exercise), and they won't spend as much of their income on good quality food. However, it's important not to be become confused between correlation and causation. The model captures the correlation between income and heart disease, but it's not right to say that having a low income necessarily causes heart disease. It might, but it could also just be acting as a proxy for those other features.

This ability to pick out new data items which are predictive, but which an expert might not have considered important before, is one of the big strengths of machine learning. This is particularly true as we move further into the world of "Big Data" where there can be tens of thousands of data items available, any one of which could feature in a predictive model – far more than could ever be analyzed by hand.

Machine learning is an automated way of sifting all those data items to find the handful that correlate with the behavior being predicted. Having said this, it's important to note that in the vast majority of cases, across many application areas, machine learning tends to pick out similar data items to what a human expert would use when making decisions. New, strange or counterintuitive predictive relationships tend to be the exception rather than the rule.

Another thing that gives predictive models an edge over human decision makers is that the scores allocated to each data item are optimal, based on the data in the development sample; i.e. the scores assigned to each data item in the model are the best they can be, resulting in the most accurate predictions possible.

Machine learning is not the only way to create scorecard type models. One alternative is to apply expert opinion. A group of experts gets together and collectively decide which factors are important and what points should be assigned to those factors. Predictive models constructed in this way often work surprisingly well but tend to be inferior to models constructed using algorithms to determine the scores using a suitable development sample.

Another interesting feature of the scorecard in Figure 2 is that it only contains 9 data items – yet that's enough to make pretty good predictions and this is often the case. Very few predictive models need more than a few dozen data items to be able to generate very good predictions indeed. Even if there are many tens of thousands of bits of data available, the vast majority of those data items add little or nothing to the accuracy of predictions. This is a very useful feature of machine learning because it means that although a huge amount of data analysis may have been required in order to create a model, far less resource is required when it comes to putting that model to use. To implement a predictive model, you only require the data items that feature in the model. No other data is required.

The scorecard model in Figure 2 predicts the likelihood of someone getting heart disease in the next 5 years. But how do the individual scores generated by the model translate into probabilities? One way to establish the relationship between score and probability is to produce a "score distribution" table as shown in Figure 3.

To produce Figure 3, a completely new sample of data, a **validation sample**, was collected for another 500,000 people (30,000 of which went on to develop heart disease over the next 5 years). This validation sample is completely independent of the sample used to construct the model[20]. It therefore gives a representative view of how the model will perform when it is applied to new people, whose details were not used to construct the model.[21]

Figure 3. A score distribution table.

Score range		Number of people	% of population	Number with heart disease after 5 yrs.	% with heart disease after 5 yrs.
From	To				
0	300	55,950	11.19%	40	0.07%
301	320	56,606	11.32%	68	0.12%
321	340	59,700	11.94%	129	0.22%
341	360	58,706	11.74%	216	0.37%
361	380	64,429	12.89%	403	0.63%
381	400	52,749	10.55%	575	1.09%
401	420	34,089	6.82%	600	1.76%
421	440	21,107	4.22%	632	2.99%
441	460	17,269	3.45%	878	5.09%
461	480	23,364	4.67%	2,020	8.65%
481	500	17,477	3.50%	2,553	14.61%
501	520	13,554	2.71%	3,366	24.84%
521	540	7,103	1.42%	3,463	48.76%
541	560	8,260	1.65%	6,587	79.74%
561	999	9,637	1.93%	8,469	87.88%
Total		500,000		30,000	6.0%

The two leftmost columns contain the score range, showing the range of scores being reported upon in each row. The first row contains details of everyone scoring 300 or less, the second row those scoring between 301 and 320 and so on. Ideally, there would be a separate row for each individual score, but because there are literally hundreds of different scores that can be generated by the model, the scores in this example have been grouped in to 20 point ranges for convenience[22].

The other columns in Figure 3 provide information about the individuals in each score range. For instance, 56,606 cases scored between 301 and 320, representing 11.32% of the cases in the validation sample. Of these, 68 went on to develop heart disease.

The rightmost column shows the percentage of people in each score range that developed heart disease. This is, in effect, the prediction made by the model. For those in the 301 – 320 score range, the model prediction is 0.12% To put it another way, anyone whose score is between 301 and 320 has about a 1 in 833 chance of developing heart disease (1/0.0012).

To evaluate the risk of a person getting heart disease in the future, all that one needs to do is:

- Calculate their score using the scorecard in Figure 2.

- Find the row into which their score falls in Figure 3.

- Look across to the rightmost column of Figure 3 to obtain a prediction.

If we return to the case of the 45 year old women who scored 404, she falls in the 401-420 score range. Reading across, the proportion of people who scored between 401 and 420 who went on to develop heart disease was 1.76%. i.e. the model predicts that she has a 1.76% (1 in 57)[23] chance of developing heart disease in the next five years.

If you have the information at hand, why not have a go at calculating your own score and coming up with a prediction for your own risk of developing heart disease?[24]

Knowing what the score means is important, but the next

question is: How well does the scorecard model predict heart disease? How accurate is it? One way to evaluate the model is to consider the differences in the rate of heart disease between the lowest and highest scoring cases. Only 0.07% of those scoring 300 or less go on to develop heart disease in the next five years. For those scoring 561 or more, 87.88% develop the condition. To put it another way, people with the highest scores are more than 1,000 times more likely to get heart disease than the people with the lowest scores – which is pretty good.

Another way to approach this is to compare the model's performance against a random selection strategy; i.e. if you select people at random for check-ups, then only 6% of those people would go on to get heart disease, whereas the best scoring group (561 - 999) performs about 15 times better than this (87.88 / 6).

Appendix A provides a more detailed explanation of the most common metrics used by data scientists to evaluate how good predictive models are at predicting behavior.

6. Using a Predictive Model to Make Decisions

By this point we:

- Have a predictive model (the scorecard of Figure 2 in the previous chapter). The model generates scores indicating how likely someone is to develop heart disease.

- Understand what the scores mean.

- Know the probability of someone getting heart disease given their score (from the information provided in Figure 3).

- Have a feel for how much better the scorecard is at identifying heart disease sufferers than a random selection policy.

- Know the distribution of the population across the range of possible scores (from the information provided in the score distribution table in Figure 3).

That's all well and good, but none of this information tells us what to do on the basis of the score that someone receives. If the model is going to provide value, then decisions need to be made and those decisions acted upon. If someone receives a score of say, 517 are they invited for a check-up or not?

Before going further, let's cast our minds back to the start of the previous chapter, where the following objective was laid out:

- Identify at least half of those who will develop heart disease in the next 5 years, and then invite them to visit their doctor for a more in-depth check-up.

Subject to the following constraint:

- No more than 5% of the population can be invited for a check-up; i.e. there are sufficient resources for 1 in every 20 people to be seen by their doctor.

To answer the question, we need to refer back to the score distribution that was introduced in Figure 3. To save you having to turn back to it, it has been reproduced as Figure 4 below.

Figure 4. Deja vu. A score distribution table (again!)

| Score range | | Number of | % of | Number with | % with heart |
From	To	people	population	heart disease after 5 yrs.	disease after 5 yrs.
0	300	55,950	11.19%	40	0.07%
301	320	56,606	11.32%	68	0.12%
321	340	59,700	11.94%	129	0.22%
341	360	58,706	11.74%	216	0.37%
361	380	64,429	12.89%	403	0.63%
381	400	52,749	10.55%	575	1.09%
401	420	34,089	6.82%	600	1.76%
421	440	21,107	4.22%	632	2.99%
441	460	17,269	3.45%	878	5.09%
461	480	23,364	4.67%	2,020	8.65%
481	500	17,477	3.50%	2,553	14.61%
501	520	13,554	2.71%	3,366	24.84%
521	540	7,103	1.42%	3,463	48.76%
541	560	8,260	1.65%	6,587	79.74%
561	999	9,637	1.93%	8,469	87.88%
Total		500,000		30,000	6.0%

The limiting factor (the constraint) in this problem is doctors' time. At most, 1 in 20 people (5%) can be invited for a check-up. Using the information from the "% of population" column in Figure 4 to do some simple arithmetic, it can be determined that:

- 1.93% of the population scores 561 or more.

- 3.58% of the population scores 541 or more.

- *5.00% of the population scores 521 or more.*

- 7.71% of the population scores 501 or more.

- And so on…

Therefore, the **cut-off strategy** (decision rule) to apply is:

- Invite anyone scoring 521 or more for a check-up and lifestyle review with their doctor.

The final step is to evaluate the impact of the decision rule. How good will the scorecard based decision-making process be? Will the model be able to identify at least 50% of heart disease sufferers within the group scoring 521 or more?

Looking at the second rightmost column in Figure 4, there are 18,519 (3,463 + 6,587 + 8,469) cases scoring 521 or more. That's 62% of the total 30,000 cases of heart disease. That's pretty good isn't it? By selecting just the 5% of the population scoring 521 or more, 62% of all heart disease cases can be identified. The objective, (to identify at least 50%) has been met.

These figures are based on the 500,000 people in the validation sample. Given that this is a large independent sample, it's a reasonably safe assumption that the results are representative of what would be observed if the model was applied to the country's entire population of many tens of millions[25].

As I've already mentioned, predictive models aren't perfect.

Some of those scoring 521 or more won't get heart disease. Using the data in the score distribution table again, it's relatively easy to work out how often the model gets it right for this particular decision rule and how often it gets it wrong, as follows:

- There are 25,000 cases scoring 521 or more.

- Of these, 18,519 get heart disease.

- The overall hit rate is therefore 74% (100 * 18,519/25,000).

- This means that while 74% of those invited are expected to develop heart disease, the remaining 26% invited for a check-up don't really need one.

The model is not perfect. It gets things wrong 26% of the time, but it's performance is far far better than selecting people at random for check-ups. With only 6% of the population expected to develop heart disease in the next five years, a random invitation strategy would result in 94% (100% – 6%) of the check-ups being wasted on people who were not going to develop heart disease in the first place.

Score distribution tables, such as those in Figure 4, underpin all of the reporting and performance metrics that support the evaluation and use of predictive models. In real world applications they tend to be much more granular (have more rows) and contain additional columns containing information such as cumulative ascending/descending numbers and percentages, to aid with calculations.

Some people, particularly old hands like me who began doing machine learning before tools like Excel were common, prefer to work directly from score distribution tables like the one in Figure 4. However, these days, there are many superb visualization tools that can be used to present the results from the score distribution table in more intuitive and user friendly ways. The best tools are also interactive. They allow you to experiment with different models, constraints and cut-off strategies to find the best decision rules for your particular problem.

Two of the most popular ways of providing a graphical representation of a score distribution table are **Lift charts** and **Gain charts**. These are described in Appendix A.

7. That's Scorecards, but What About Decision Trees?

Decision trees are another popular type of predictive model. Like scorecards, they are also very easy to understand and use.

To demonstrate what decision trees look like and how they work, let's continue with the problem of heart disease. If you recall, the objective is to find a way to identify at least half of those who will develop heart disease, but to invite no more than 1 in 20 (5%) of the population for a check-up with their doctor.

To build a decision tree model, the 500,000 cases that were used to build the scorecard are used again, but this time a different type of algorithm is applied to the development sample. All popular decision tree algorithms are variations on the theme of repeatedly splitting the development sample into smaller and smaller groups. The following is a simple description of a decision tree algorithm:

Step 1. Pick one data item in the development sample (e.g. income).

Step 2. Find the value of income which results in the best partitioning of the data into two parts. By "best" I mean a low income group and high income group such that the incidence of heart disease is maximized in one group and minimized in the other[26].

Step 3. Repeat steps 1 and 2 for all other data items in the development sample (i.e. replace income with age, BMI, smoker etc.)

Step 4. From what has been found in steps 2 and 3, split the development sample into two parts using the best partition found; i.e. split the development sample such that the incidence of heart disease is maximized in one split and minimized in the other.

Step 5. Repeat steps 1-4 for each of the two resulting parts of the development sample. Keep doing this until no more significant differences can be found from further splitting.

Figure 5 shows the structure of a decision tree model derived from the heart disease development sample, once all the splitting criteria have been applied.

Figure 5. A decision tree model.

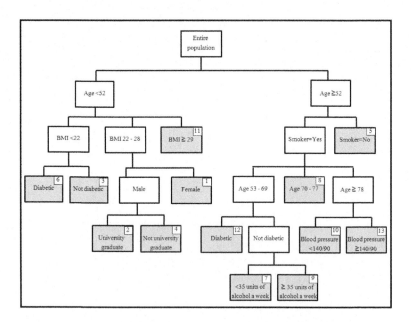

In Figure 5, the algorithm has begun by identifying that the most significant variable is age. The development sample is segmented based on if someone is greater or less than 52 years old. For those aged less than 52, the algorithm has then determined that the next most significant split is based on BMI. However, for those aged 52 or more, the next most important variable is if someone is a smoker, and so on.

To calculate a score for someone using the decision tree, one starts at the top of the tree at the first node (Entire population). One then moves down the tree. At each branching point the node is chosen that fits that person's individual characteristics. If someone is less than 52 years old the left hand side of the tree is followed. If they are aged 52 years or more then the right hand branch is followed. The process is repeated at each decision point until there are no further decisions to be made. The final node in the tree (called an end node or leaf node) into which a person falls determines their score.

In Figure 5, there are 13 end nodes (shaded in grey and numbered) and hence 13 scores that someone can receive. Those scoring 1 have the lowest chance of developing heart disease, those scoring 13 the highest.

In terms of how the scores generated by the decision tree are used, the process is virtually identical to the way one would use the scores from the scorecard. The details of the 500,000 people from the validation sample are run through the decision tree to obtain scores, and a score distribution table is then produced showing how the scores are distributed. Figure 6 shows the score distribution table for the decision tree.

Going through the same process that we followed for the scorecard, the highest scoring 5% of the population is covered by those scoring 12 or 13. Of these, 16,910 subsequently go on to develop heart disease, which is 55% of the total number of cases. Therefore, the targeting strategy for inviting people for a check-up is to invite all those scoring 12 or 13.

Like the scorecard, this strategy also meets the stated objective of inviting no more than 5% of the total population for a check-up, but having at least half of those who will go on to develop heart disease within that 5%

Figure 6. Score distribution for the decision tree model.

Node (Score)	Number of people	% of population	Number with heart disease after 5 yrs.	% with heart disease after 5 yrs.
1	98,760	19.75%	109	0.11%
2	104,324	20.86%	177	0.17%
3	32,176	6.44%	93	0.29%
4	78,287	15.66%	385	0.49%
5	19,998	4.00%	162	0.81%
6	28,675	5.74%	460	1.60%
7	48,748	9.75%	1,581	3.24%
8	22,801	4.56%	1,491	6.54%
9	18,884	3.78%	2,452	12.98%
10	15,034	3.01%	3,419	22.74%
11	7,313	1.46%	2,763	37.78%
12	18,901	3.78%	11,889	62.90%
13	6,099	1.22%	5,021	82.32%
Total	500,000		30,000	6.0%

OK. We now have two models. The question that will now be on many peoples' lips is: which is the best model? Is it the scorecard or the decision tree? When people ask this question, what they usually want to know is: which model generates the most accurate predictions?

In this example, both models provided sufficient predictive accuracy to meet the stated objective. However, the scorecard is better. The reason why it's better is because if you use the scorecard to decide which 5% of the population to invite for a check-up (those scoring 521 or more), you would expect to invite 62% of those who go on to develop heart disease. The decision tree on the other hand only identifies 55% of them (those scoring 12 or 13).

At this point it's worth making some observations about the similarities and differences between the decision tree model and the scorecard model. Some important things to note are:

- The decision tree and scorecard use similar, but not identical, data items to make their predictions. The scorecard includes annual income but the decision tree does not. "Graduate" features in the decision tree model but not the scorecard.

- The branch conditions in the decision tree don't always align with the score ranges in the scorecard. In the scorecard, age breaks occur at 49 and 57, but in the decision tree, the key age split is at 52 years old (with additional age splits further down the tree).

- The decision tree generates 13 possible scores, whereas there are hundreds of scores that can be generated by the scorecard; i.e. the scorecard generates a much more granular range of scores than the decision tree.

The fact that the scorecard and decision tree models have differences in the data that they use is a feature of the algorithms used to construct them. There are literally hundreds of different machine learning algorithms that can be used to construct many different types of predictive models. Each algorithm has its own logic for selecting which data items are important predictors and the weights those predictors should be given in the model. Each approach has its strengths and weakness and is better at predicting some types of cases than others.

What this means in practice is that there no such thing as a best type of model that should always be used for all types of problem. No one type of predictive model can be said to be universally better than all the others. The scorecard proved to be better (in terms of predictive accuracy) than the decision tree this time, but for a different type of problem, using different data and with different objectives, it may be the case that a decision tree wins out.

This means is that if you want to ensure that you get the very best model for your particular problem (as measured in terms of predictive accuracy), you have to build different models, compare them against each other, and then decide which one is the most appropriate.

Having said this, in practical real-world situations, most types of model yield very similar levels of predictive performance for many types of problem[27]. There may be theoretical arguments as to why one type of model is better than another, or why Algorithm A is superior to Algorithm B, but in practice they are all much of a muchness in many application areas. Therefore, there is a good deal of latitude that can be applied when selecting which type of model to choose.

This is another great feature of machine learning. This is because it means that other factors, in addition to predictive accuracy, can come into play when deciding which model is best for a given problem. In particular, in some problem domains, having a model that is easily explicable and which is aligned to a common-sense view as to how decisions should be made is vital. This is sometimes far more important than having a model that is theoretically more appropriate or marginally more accurate, but which is less well understood by business users or industry regulators.

8. Neural Networks and Deep Learning

Our brains contain billions upon billions of neurons, each interconnected to yield trillions of connections. It's the combination of neurons and the connections between them that drive our ability to think and act intelligently, to understand how the world works and to make decisions (both consciously and unconsciously) about how we interact with the world.

Back in the 1950s, computer scientists first came up with the concept of the "Artificial Neuron[28]", but it wasn't until the mid-1980s that using multiple artificial neurons linked together (a **neural network**[29]) was proposed as a way of solving complex problems[30]. Since that time, the popularity of neural networks has continued to grow and advanced forms of neural networks are currently at the forefront of research into artificial intelligence and machine learning.

The first thing to say about neural networks is that while they are sometimes touted as being immensely complex "brain like" things, they can be readily understood if one is willing to spend a little time and effort to study them. It's certainly true that a typical neural network is more complex than the scorecards and decision trees that were introduced in previous chapters, but the underlying principles are not that much different at the end of the day – there is just more of it.

To illustrate the operation of neural networks, we shall return once more to the heart disease prediction problem that we have used before. To begin, let's start with the building block of a neural network – the neuron. A **neuron** in machine learning terms is not a living thing that's been grown by a mad scientist in a covert lab somewhere, but is a simple and simplistic representation of how natural neurons behave, created using equations implemented as computer code. Figure 7 provides an illustration of how an artificial neuron works.

Figure 7. An artificial neuron.

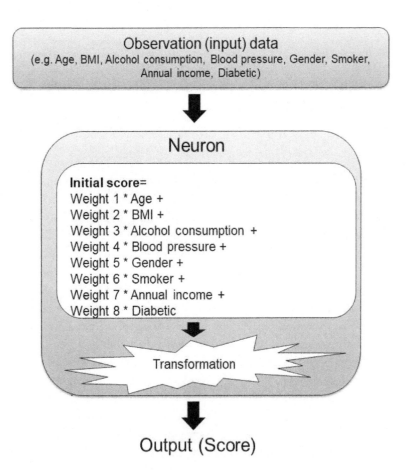

The operation of the neuron in Figure 7 is as follows:

1. The observation data, such as Age and BMI, provides the inputs to the neuron.

2. Each input is multiplied by a weight (which can be positive or negative). For non-numeric data such as gender or smoker, 0/1 flags are used to represent each condition. For example, 1 if female, 0 if male.

3. The inputs, multiplied by their weights, are added up to get an initial score.

4. After the initial score has been calculated it is transformed. Often this is to force the score to be in the range 0-1. This transformation is not absolutely essential but is deemed "good practice." This is so that when the neuron is combined with others to produce a neural network, all the neurons produce values in the same range; i.e. between 0 and 1.

5. The transformed version of the initial score is the output score produced by the neuron.

So, a neuron in the context of machine learning isn't anything mysterious or complex, it's just a couple of simple formulas. The first multiplies each of the input variables by a weight and adds up the total. The second formula (called an **activation function**[1] in data science speak) then modifies (transforms) this value so that it lies within a fixed range, usually between 0 and 1. It's as simple as that! The clever bit is determining what the weights should be, which we will cover shortly.

On its own, a single neuron is really not that much different from a scorecard type model. The only material difference is the transformation to force the score to lie in a fixed range. It fact, it can

---

[1] I promised no complex formulas, but I'll throw just one into the mix. There are many activation functions, but a very common one is the "logistic function." This is calculated as $1/(1+e^{-(\text{Initial Score})})$. The value of e is 2.718. e is a bit like PI (3.142) in that it appears in all sorts of places in mathematics and statistics.

be proven that the outputs generated by neuron and a scorecard type model are equivalent[31].

To produce a neural network model a number of neurons are connected together. Figure 8 provides an example of how this occurs.

Figure 8. A neural network model.

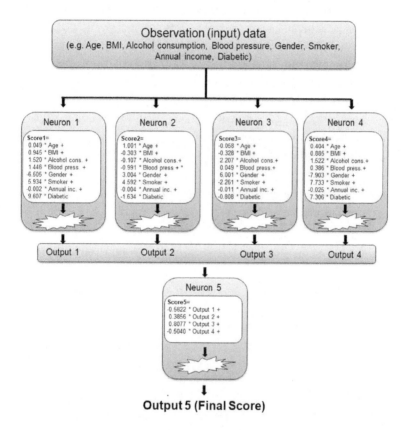

Output 5 (Final Score)

In Figure 8, the input data is supplied to each of the four neurons in the first layer. Each neuron has its own independent set of weights. The weights, when combined with the input data, create base scores

(Score1, Score2, etc.). These scores are then transformed to create four outputs. The outputs from this first layer of neurons provides the inputs to the single neuron in the second layer (Neuron 5). Neuron 5 then multiplies each of the outputs from the first 4 neurons by a weight to create Score5. This is then transformed to create the final score from the network. The key features of the neural network in Figure 8 are:

- The inputs to each neuron in a given layer are the same (e.g. Age, BMI etc. for the first layer neurons), but the weights within each neuron are different. Therefore, each neuron produces a different score.

- The outputs (the scores) from the first set of neurons (the first layer) provide the inputs to the second set of neurons (the second layer).

- There are four neurons in the first layer in this example. In practice, the optimal number of neurons can't be determined up front. Instead, a number of competing models are built with different numbers of neurons, and the one that performs the best is chosen. A rule of thumb that works well for most business applications is to have between half and double the number of input data items (so between 4 and 16 in this example).

- There are lots of weights. Figure 8 is a very simple network. It has just 8 input variables and 5 neurons, but there are 36 weights. A typical business application with say, 100 input variables and 75 neurons, would have 7,474 weights[32].

Once a neural network has been created it can be assessed and used in the same way as scorecards and decision trees; i.e. scores are created for a validation sample, which is then used to produce score distribution tables such those in Figures 3 and 6. These are then used to derive decision rules about what to do with cases given the score that they receive.

The collection of weights in the network represent the patterns that the **training algorithm** has identified. So how does the training algorithm determine what the weights should be? There are many different algorithms that have been created to find the weights in a neural network, but they all tend to adopt the following principles:

1. Assign each weight a random or zero value.

2. Calculate the scores generated by the network for all of the cases in the development sample.

3. Assess how accurate the final score is. For example, by assessing the lift and gain properties of the model, as detailed in Appendix A.

4. Adjust the weights so as to improve the predictive accuracy of the model.

5. Repeat steps 1-4 until no further significant improvement in model performance is observed, or a certain amount of time has elapsed.

The clever bit is in Step 4, how one adjusts the weights. The simplest approach is just to randomly try different values and see what works best. However, this is very inefficient and is unlikely to yield a good solution in realistic time. All practical neural network training algorithms are cleverer than this. They adopt a variety of different weight adjustment strategies based on the differences in performance between each iteration of the algorithm. They will make big adjustments to the weights at the start of the process when it's easy to obtain large improvements in predictive performance, and then gradually make smaller changes as performance improves so as to home in on the optimum solution.

The neural network in Figure 8 has a single neuron in the second layer (Neuron 5) which generates a single score. This score represents the likelihood of someone having a heart attack in the next 5 years. If the network was being used for a problem where there were multiple events being predicted then there would be a separate neuron to represent each event. For problems such as object recognition, there could be hundreds or even thousands of scores being generated by the neurons in the final layer. Each score would represent the probability of the item being one particular object. The object associated with the highest score would then be taken as the prediction generated by the system.

The reason why neural networks are so popular is their ability to detect subtle patterns in data which other simpler methods, such as scorecards and decision trees, may not be able to detect. This means that they can potentially produce more accurate predictions. This is achieved by having the two layers of neurons, with the scores from the first layer providing the inputs to the second layer.

The main drawback of neural networks is that the scores that they generate are not intuitive. Yes, one can see what the various weights in the model are and understand the overall score calculation, but if I was to ask you which input variable in Figure 8 contributes the most to the final score, then this is much less obvious than for the scorecard and decision tree models of heart disease. This is potentially a problem if there is a business or legal requirement to explain how the final model score was arrived at.

Deep learning represents the latest evolution of neural network type models. The neural network in Figure 8 has two layers of neurons and this structure is used very successfully in many traditional neural network applications. However, there is no reason why there can't be many more layers. Consider the network in Figure 9. It has the same initial inputs as the network in Figure 8. There is also a single output neuron (Neuron 13) which delivers the final model score. However, the network in Figure 9 has 4 layers of neurons compared to just 2 layers in Figure 8.

In theory, there is no reason why the network could not be extended even further. There could be 5, 6, 7, ..., 100+ layers if desired, with different numbers of neurons in each layer. What one tends to find is that as more layers are added, so the ability of the network to identify complex and/or subtle patterns increases. The more layers the "deeper" the network. Generally speaking, anything with more than 2 or 3 layers can be classified as a "deep" network, but there is no single accepted definition.

Figure 9. A deep neural network model.

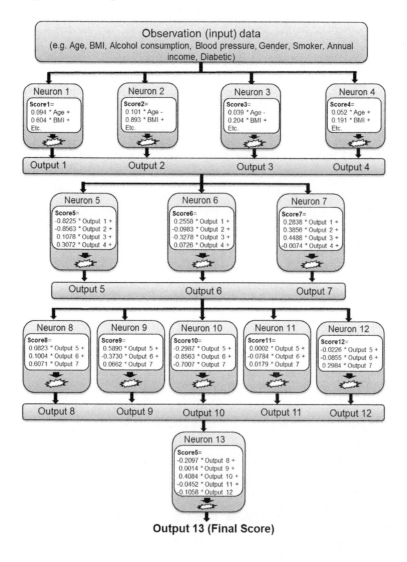

As well as expanding the number of neurons and layers in a network, other avenues of research associated with deep learning consider how the neurons in the network are connected. In a standard network, as in Figures 8 and 9, all of the neurons in each layer are connected to all of the neurons in the next layer. However, other configurations are possible. For example, not connecting all inputs to all of the neurons in the first layer (a **convoluted neural network**). This works particularly well for certain types of problem such as image recognition[33].

Another variant on standard neural networks is to create feedback loops such that the outputs of neurons in later layers act as inputs to earlier layers (a **recurrent neural network**). This makes it possible to incorporate latency, to provide a representation of time, which is not captured by traditional machine learning approaches.

What this means in practice, is that recurrent neural networks work well when information is contained in a sequence of events within the development sample used to train the network. If you are using machine learning to decipher handwriting one letter at a time, the fact that the previous letter in a word was say, the letter "Z" will be an important predictor for the next letter, which is almost certainly a vowel or the letter "S." A traditional neural network for handwriting recognition would not consider these sequential relationships. Google translate is one example of a commercial product that uses recurrent networks.

The most complex neural network models in use today, such as the ones developed by Google's DeepMind subsidiary to beat the world's best Go players[34], combine these features and have millions of neurons connected across dozens of layers.

Complex deep learning models, based on neural networks, are driving many sophisticated artificial intelligence applications, but for many types of problems this is overkill. A very complex model is only required for a very complex problem. It's the old adage: "You don't need a sledgehammer to crack a nut." In fact, if you try to apply a very complex machine learning approach to a very simple problem, then sometimes what you actually get is a worse result than if a very simple model is used. This may seem counter intuitive, but there will be a tendency for the model to find false patterns that don't really exist, whereas this is less likely with simple models.

One way that I try and think about these issues is to consider if things can be thought of as either a "simple" or "complex" type of prediction/AI problem:

- **"Simple" AI problems.** These have a singular objective or thing that one is trying to determine, which is easy to quantify. For a classification problem, this means that the outcome can be expressed as a simple "Yes" or "No" such as does someone default on a loan or not? For a regression problem, can the outcome be expressed as single number? Such as how much someone spent in store the last time they shopped.

- **"Complex" AI problems**. These usually have multiple and very nuanced objectives. Classic examples of "complex" problems are object recognition, language translation and game playing (e.g. chess or Go). This also includes problems that require multiple machine learning approaches to be used in combination, such as in autonomous vehicles and digital personal assistants.

It's not always as clear cut as this, but as a rule of thumb it's not a bad place to start.

Most business applications that you are likely to come across (target marketing, credit scoring, who to hire/fire, matching on dating sites, etc.) fall into the "Simple AI" category. A network with a couple of hundred neurons spread over just two layers is more than enough and will probably yield similar or marginally better performance than a well-designed scorecard type model. However, you can never be sure. As with other aspects of machine learning, the advice to whoever is building predictive models for you is to try out a number of different approaches and then see which one satisfies your requirements the best. This is both in terms of raw predictive accuracy and business requirements/constraints. If there is a business or legal requirement for the model outputs to be explicable to a layperson, can you explain in simple terms why the model came up with the score that it did?

A data scientist should always use a simple approach such as a scorecard as an initial benchmark, and then try to improve upon that using more complex/advanced methods.

9. Unsupervised and Reinforcement Learning

The machine learning techniques we have discussed so far have assumed that there is a development sample which contains both observation data and outcome data. For the heart disease problem, each patient's data in the development sample was labeled to identify if they subsequently went on to develop heart disease. The application of various machine learning algorithms was described to find the relationships that exist between the observation and outcome data. These relationships were then captured in the form of a model such as a scorecard, a decision tree or a neural network. The resulting model could then be used to predict the probability of people developing heart disease in the future, based on what is known about them today.

Machine learning applied to labeled data; where each case in the development sample has both observation and outcome data, is referred to as **supervised learning**. The vast majority of AI/machine learning applications that you will come across in the business world such as target marketing, fraud detection and employee vetting are examples of supervised learning. If you have labeled data available, then a supervised approach is usually the right one to follow and will yield the best results.

There are however, certain types of problem where outcome data is very limited or does not exist – there is only unlabeled observation data. Therefore, while this book is mainly about supervised learning, it's worth spending some time considering what can be done in such situations.

When outcome data is not available, a set of techniques referred to as **unsupervised learning** can be applied. A key feature of unsupervised learning is that it is primarily used for knowledge discovery; that is, detecting interesting features in data. This contrasts with supervised learning which is usually associated with predicting an outcome using the matching observation data.

What this means in practice, is that unsupervised learning approaches are great at helping to identify and group things based on similarities between them, but they do not provide you with predictions that tell you how someone or something is going to behave. The objectives and outputs from supervised and unsupervised learning, are therefore, very different. With supervised learning, the end game is a predictive model of some sort. The model can then be used to predict the behaviour of new cases when they present themselves. With unsupervised learning, the output is a representation of the structure of the data which is a different thing altogether.

The most common type of unsupervised learning in use today is **clustering**[35]. The goal of clustering is to identify similarities and/or connections within data such that you can group (cluster) similar cases together. The idea is that because cases in a given cluster have a lot of very similar attributes, then you can treat everyone in that cluster in a similar way.

To illustrate clustering in action, consider Rebecca, the manager of a cinema complex located in a university town. Most of her customers attend shows at evenings and weekends. This is presumably because they are at work or school the rest of the time. However, she does provide some early bird shows mid-week, even though these shows are not very well attended. What Rebecca would like to do is understand more about the types of people who attend these mid-week shows. She can then target promotional offers at similar people in the local community, who might be interested in watching a film at that time, and hence improve the cinema's audience figures.

This is an unsupervised problem because Rebecca has no information about how people have responded to marketing activity previously. There isn't a list of people who were sent promotional offers in the past and a corresponding flag (label) indicating if they took up the offer or not. This rules out developing any type of predictive model built using a supervised learning approach.

Rebecca does however, know who in the local community has been to the cinema recently. This is because these days, most people leave a record of their attendance via the payment method they used or location information from their smartphone. Once you have that, then a whole host of other information about those people can be obtained from a variety of sources.

Two pieces of information that she thinks are particularly relevant are the age of filmgoers and how far from the cinema they live. Figure 10 shows a plot of these two items for a random sample of early bird customers.

Figure 10. Age and distance from the cinema.

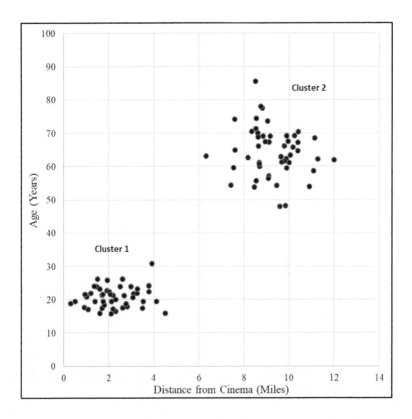

From Figure 10 two groupings (clusters) are clearly visible. Younger people who live close by and older people, predominately of retirement age, who live some distance away.

It's apparent from Figure 10 that there are very few younger customers who live more than a short distance from the cinema. Also, the age range of those in cluster 1 is quite narrow; it's almost entirely late teens to mid-twenties. Another interesting feature of Figure 10 is that there is almost nobody aged between thirty and fifty attending any of the early bird performances.

Rebecca does not know why the clusters appear in the way that they do, but she hazards a guess that younger cinema goers are predominately college students with gaps in their teaching schedules. They may also rely more on public transport, making it less convenient to travel a long way to get to the cinema. Likewise, the old folks probably have more flexibility in their day than the average person, have more time on their hands, have a car and are willing to travel further. They also tend to live in larger houses out in the suburbs, compared to students who tend to live in university accommodation nearer the cinema.

Although very simple, the information in Figure 10 can help Rebecca formulate a marketing strategy tailored to each of the two customer groups. This could be in terms of:

- What films individuals in each group are targeted with.

- Travel offers reflecting different modes of transport used to get to the cinema.

- Discounts on extras that are likely to appeal to each group (maybe soda/beer for younger people and coffee/tea/wine for the seniors).

Equally importantly, Rebecca knows that the early bird cinema audiences contain very few people of "middle age." Hence, she should not waste her marketing budget trying to persuade them to come to the cinema.

The cinema scenario illustrates the concept of clustering in a very simple way, using just two items of information. The same principles can be applied when there are hundreds or thousands of data items available about people, but it's just not very easy to represent the clusters graphically once you have more than 2 or 3 items of data[36]. Finding out how many clusters there are in the data and what the features of those clusters are, is a fundamental part of the clustering process.

There are many commercial products based on clustering. Experian's Mosaic product assigns all 1.8 million postcodes (zip codes) in the UK[37] to one of 66 clusters. Experian gives each cluster a title such as "Uptown elite", "Low income workers" and "Classic grandparents" to represent the types of people who typically live in those areas. Geo-demographic information about the average age, wealth, number of kids, credit usage and so on is provided for the inhabitants living in the postcodes of each cluster. Organizations then tailor their customer engagement strategy to match the demographics of the people in each postcode. This works because people living in households in the same neighborhood tend to have similar demographics. If you are a highly paid banker living in an area classified as "Uptown elite" then it's far more likely that your neighbors are also highly paid professionals as opposed to families surviving on benefits or the minimum wage.

Many clustering algorithms are based on the principle of minimizing the *distance* between cases in the development sample. *Distance* in this instance doesn't necessarily refer to physical distance, but how different two cases are for a given data item. The distance between two individuals aged 22 and 24 is less than that between two people aged 18 and 75. If we are talking about smoking habits, then two smokers have a distance of zero whereas a smoker and a non-smoker don't. The distance between two people within the same pay grade is typically less than the distance between two people on different pay grades and so on.

Before a clustering algorithm is applied, each data item in the development sample is transformed to a standard numerical scale. For example, ages and incomes could both be transformed so that the average value of each was zero, and most cases lie between the values of -1 and +1[38]. Likewise, 0/1 indicators are used to represent things such as if someone is a smoker or not. In this way, the differences for each data item all carry equal weight when the clustering algorithm is applied. If this standardization process does not occur, then the influence of data items with a large scale such as income in dollars, will dwarf those with much smaller values such as number of dependents.

There are many different clustering algorithms available, but one of the most popular is called **K-means clustering.** This is the type of clustering Experian describe using in the design of their Mosaic Product[39].

The K-means clustering algorithm works to assign every case in your sample to one of K distinct clusters, where K is a value selected by the user[40]. The algorithm does this by assigning cases to clusters so that the sum of all the individual distances within each of the clusters is minimized.

With clustering there isn't a model that is produced at the end of the process. All there is, is an identifier to say which of the K clusters an observation has been assigned to. You may be placed in cluster 4, but I on the other hand, have been assigned to cluster 7. When there are new cases which need to be assigned to a cluster, one of two approaches can be adopted.

1. The clustering algorithm is rerun. The clusters are reassigned with the new cases included.

2. The distance between each of the new case and the center[41] of each cluster is calculated. Cases are assigned to the cluster whose centers they are closest too.

The first option is optimal in terms of cluster assignment because the clusters will evolve over time as more cases are presented. However, clustering can require a lot of computer power. If the cases need to be assigned in (near) real time, option 2 is more practical. Let's illustrate this with an example, as shown in Figure 11.

Figure 11. Assigning cases to clusters.

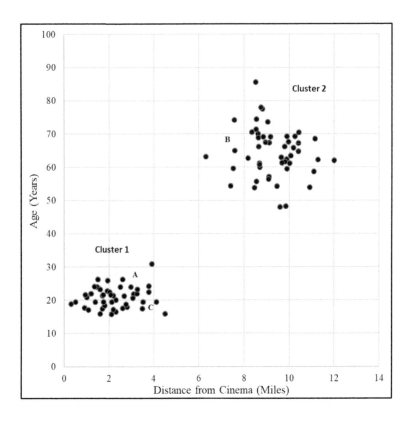

In Figure 11 the letters A, B and C represent new customers who are to be assigned to one of the two clusters already identified. Once they have been assigned to a cluster, then Rebecca can target them with the appropriate marketing activity. It's easy to see that customers A and C are closer to cluster 1, whereas customer B is closest to cluster 2. The sum of distances within the clusters will be minimized if A and C are assigned to cluster 1 and customer B to cluster 2.

Customer profiling applied to marketing is one of the of the best known applications of clustering, but clustering based approaches are also being applied successfully to many other problems. One example is document clustering. In fields such as law and academic research, there is a requirement to regularly trawl through the ever-growing pile of published literature to find information relating to certain subjects or types of research. Some fields of study cover millions of papers and articles. The mathematics database zbMATH contains about 4 million entries with reviews or abstracts from 3,000 journals and 180,000 books[42]. In medicine, more than 800,000 academic papers are published each year[43]. The traditional of way of searching for documents is similar to using Google or Bing – one types keywords into the database's search engine, which finds papers that match those keywords. However, search terms don't necessarily bring back all of the relevant documents and many are returned which are not relevant but contain the keywords in a different context. Some documents, particularly older ones, may not have any keywords associated with them or use different terminology, which means they are missed in the search.

Document clustering is in essence no different from the cinema example we talked about earlier. Instead of geo-demographics; word counts, sentence structure and other document features provide the data items used in the clustering process.

Document clustering can also be applied to tweets, newsfeeds, blog posts and other rapidly changing media in real time. Pictures and video can also be categorized in a similar way. News organizations use these approaches to automatically flag up new posts about specific topics as they appear. This is so that they can include them in their own media publications almost immediately. Social media companies and governments use similar methods (as well as predictive models) to support the identification of illegal or undesirable content.

Supervised learning approaches work very well when there is a large amount of observation data and each observation has a clear unambiguous outcome. If there are no outcomes available, then unsupervised learning can sometimes prove useful; albeit in a somewhat different context. There are however, problems where there may be no observation or outcome data initially, but the learning process is able to assess its performance on a case-by-case basis as it goes. The model is adjusted each time, based on some measure of success or reward, which is calculated each time a task is attempted. This type of machine learning is called **reinforcement learning**.

A somewhat over-simplistic example of reinforcement learning is training a neural network to find the highest point in the local terrain using the least number of steps possible. At the start, all one knows is the current map location (longitude, latitude and height above sea level). The network can generate 4 possible scores, each representing a move forward, backwards left or right. The current state of being; i.e. the current location, provides the input (observation data). The resulting state of being, i.e. the new location after the move suggested by the network has been executed, is the outcome.

After each move, the new state of being is assessed. Are we now in a better position (higher above sea level) than before? If the answer is yes, then the algorithm is deemed to have done well - the measure of reward or success is high. If not, then the algorithm is deemed to have performed poorly – the measure of success is low. The algorithm then adjusts the model weights based on the degree of success that its action has resulted in.

A more refined version of this algorithm would also consider past movement history; i.e. where it has been, as part of the input data. It would also make sense to include a longer term view of future success rather than just the one move ahead position. For example, penalizing the success if the same location is visited more than once or providing a reward (increased success) for entering new, unexplored areas of the terrain even if the initial move into that area does not find a higher point initially.

Data scientists will often talk about their being three distinct types of machine learning; i.e. supervised, unsupervised and reinforcement learning. However, reinforcement learning shares a lot of features with supervised learning. As with supervised learning the algorithms used in reinforcement learning deliver a model, typically based on some form of neural network. Likewise, the model is adjusted based on an assessment of outcomes that results from a given set of input data. As more iterations of the algorithm occur and the weights in the model are refined so the model's performance improves.

The terms "reward/success" and "failure/penalty" tend to be applied to reinforcement learning, but these are very similar concepts to "accuracy" and "error" that are used to describe how well a predictive model, developed using supervised learning, performs. A small error between actual and predicted values in supervised learning; i.e. a very accurate prediction, is broadly equivalent to a high degree success in reinforcement learning. In the same way, an incorrect classification or inaccurate prediction in supervised learning is analogous to low reward/failure in reinforcement learning.

A great example of the difference between supervised and reinforcement learning is how model training occurs to create a chess playing program. A supervised approach would take thousands of game moves (or sequence of moves) from previously played games as the observation data, with the labeled outcome data providing an indication of if the move was a good one or not. The scores produced by the model are used to indicate which piece to move and to where. The algorithm then finds the model weights that result in the overall best set of moves, measured against the moves contained in the development sample.

With reinforcement learning, no data is provided initially – none at all! The model scores still indicate which move to make just like the supervised approach. However, initially these will be more or less random, given that there is no data to train the model against. Each time a move is made the status of the board (the new state of being) is re-evaluated. The algorithm then adjusts the weights in the model based on how successful its move was deemed to be.

Evaluating how successful a move is in chess is complex and will often incorporate probable future states of being as well as the current one. However, for the purposes of this example, a simple success criteria is the difference in the value of each players' pieces remaining on the board after a move has been made[44]. If your move results in the taking of a high value piece, but not losing one yourself, then that's a strong success. Making a move and then having one of your pieces taken is a failure, yielding a low measure of success. The ultimate success or failure is losing one's king – checkmate. In this way, by assessing each move and adjusting the model weights accordingly, the program learns by itself without needing to be supplied with any prior information.

A key advantage that reinforcement learning has over supervised learning is that there is no limit to the set of moves that can be explored as the algorithm modifies the weights in the model. With supervised learning, you are limited to the labeled examples available in the development sample. For a game like chess, even a huge development sample, containing all the moves and outcomes from millions of games, will contain only a very tiny proportion of all possible moves. This was demonstrated very effectively when Google's DeepMind AI team used two reinforcement algorithms to play against each other. Not only did the resulting model outperform the best existing chess program at the time, but during the process the algorithm discovered completely new strategies of play, previously unknown to human grandmasters[45].

Reinforcement learning has generated a lot of excitement because the learning process is very much like the way living beings learn. If I'm trying to learn to juggle then I don't have any information to begin with. I try, I fail, I try and fail again, I try and I manage to juggle for couple of seconds, and before you know it I'm juggling like a pro! With each attempt my brain is subconsciously learning more about its environment and refining its actions based on each success or failure; i.e. the length of time I've been able to keep the balls in the air without dropping them.

Reinforcement learning has potential, but it does have its weakness and is better suited to some tasks than others. One issue is that the training algorithm is bounded by the speed of the trial and error process. If a reinforcement algorithm is being trained to make mortgage lending decisions, then the time between an action being taken and the assessment of how successful that action was could be months or years. Consequently, the training process will take far too long to be of practical use.

Deciding who to lend money too is a far simpler problem than chess and there is usually a lot of labeled development data available. Therefore, you will get better results much more quickly with a supervised approach for problems like credit risk assessment. The same issue applies to any type of problem where success cannot be measured very quickly. If we return to the chess example, the DeepMind chess playing program needed to play 68 million games to become as good as it did. It could only do this by playing against another computer, allowing games to be played in a fraction of a second. It could not have achieved the same results in a reasonable amount of time if it had been playing against human competitors in the real world. The training process would have been far too slow.

Another weakness of reinforcement learning is the cost of failure during the training process. If you embed a reinforcement learning algorithm into your organization's recruitment policy, then you are going to get a lot of terrible hires initially which is going to cause all sorts of problems. In a similar vein, you wouldn't want to connect a reinforcement learning algorithm directly to the controls of a passenger airliner[46].

OK, so finding the tops of fictional hilltops and being superhuman at chess is all very well, but what are the real-world business applications of reinforcement learning? To be honest, not a huge number at the moment. Personally, I've never been involved in delivering a solution that used it and I don't know anyone who has. I've also done a fair amount of research and found a lot of very interesting academic papers and enthusiastic press articles, but far fewer real world examples. My conclusion is that the number of reinforcement learning based solutions in use today is tiny compared to the number of supervised leaning ones. If I had to put a figure on it, I'd guess that more than 95% of real world application utilize supervised learning and most of the remaining 5% are unsupervised approaches based on clustering. However, that may change in time as the technology matures. Intuitively, if you have algorithms that can build something that plays chess or Go better than any living person, then they must have potential in other areas.

One area where reinforcement learning looks like having an impact, is in improving the efficiency of sophisticated control systems in uncertain or chaotic environments. Complex systems such as power grids, heating systems and server farms, have lots of controls which are adjusted to manage different parts the system. The relationship between the controls and the performance of the system is not always obvious. It's not a simple case of one control impacts just one thing – everything is interconnected. Tweaking the water pressure in the cooling system of a power plant to improve turbine performance has a negative impact on the efficiency of a transformer further down the line. Just like the chess problem, where there is an almost infinite number of possible games that can be played, in a power plant there are an almost infinite number of combinations of control settings. Reinforcement learning finds better ways of setting the controls through trial and error, to optimize the overall efficiency of the system. This mirrors the way an experienced engineer would use their knowledge and intuition, learnt over many years of practice, as to what the system wide effects of tweaking different controls are likely to be.

Another area where reinforcement learning is showing promise is in robotics. This is to train robots to carry out complex manual task that could previously only be undertaken by a trained person. A robotic device is given the task of doing something like flipping burgers, sorting items or stacking shelves, and through trial and error they can potentially learn to do this very effectively.

10. How to Build a Predictive Model

In this chapter we are going to melt through the keyhole to the other side... We'll cross the boundary from the sane and sensible world of the everyday into the twisted multi-dimensional realm of the data scientist; i.e. technical specialists with mathematics degrees and PhDs. On our journey we are going to:

1. Describe the process that a data scientist should follow when applying machine learning to develop predictive models, which are then going to be used as part of an automated decision-making system.

2. Explain this process in a way that a normal person can understand. This is to help you keep tabs on what the data scientists are doing. This in turn will ensure that you get what you have asked for rather than what the data scientist *thinks* your organization needs.

As we discussed right at the start of the book, the AI/machine learning projects that tend to succeed are those where business users and data scientists work hand-in-hand. In my experience, when data scientists have been left to "just get on with it" and deliver results as a coup de grâce at the end of the project, what tends to be delivered are sub-optimal solutions. In the worst case, they may fail to deliver anything useful at all.

The vast majority of the data scientists I've worked with are very conscious of the need to involve their clients in the machine learning process and have worked hard to get business input to their projects. However, it's sad to say that I have also seen more than one instance of deliberate attempts by data scientists to confuse normal people with tech speak or have avoided speaking to them all together. This is so that they can get on with all the important mathsy stuff without having to deal with those awful business people who actually have to run the organization on a day-to-day basis. When trying to establish if a data scientist is doing their job, a very simple rule to follow is:

- If they can't explain to you in plain English what they are doing and why, then they have failed in their task.

Data scientists also need to provide the business with a clear understanding of the real-world impacts of their work. As a business user, I have no interest in the fact that a predictive model is 95% accurate or that it is 10% more discriminatory than the process it's going to replace. What I want to know is: how much money is the model going to make me, how many lives is it going to save, how many less staff will I need to employ, or whatever it is that's going to impact my business objectives. It's a poor data scientist who can't express the merits of their solution in terms of the bottom line benefits it provides to their client.

However, it works both ways. It's not fair to lay everything on the data scientists. It's not an unreasonable ask that business users make an effort to gain a basic understanding of how a data scientist goes about the machine learning process. As projects progress, there should be two-way exchanges of information and regular meetings where preliminary findings and results, problems and issues are presented and discussed in a non-technical business focused way. This then guides how the project is taken forward.

With this in mind, I'm going to avoid going into the mathematics of various algorithms used for machine learning such as those used to train neural networks or decide how the splits in decision trees are assigned. For those of you who are interested in the technical details, the most common algorithms used for machine learning are all pretty well documented (see Appendix B for some recommended books and internet sites). Likewise, the implementation of these algorithms are available in commercial statistics packages that you can buy or are freely available via open source software (e.g. R and Python code libraries). You don't need to know how to code up specific machine learning algorithms; you just need to know how to call the relevant function or procedure in your chosen software package.

Figure 12 outlines the key steps in the machine learning process to develop a predictive model.

Figure 12. The machine learning process.

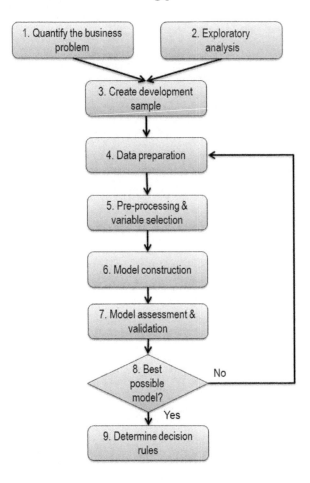

The first thing the data scientist needs to do is to quantify the business problem (Step 1); i.e. to represent what the business is trying to achieve as a simple number or score. The sales director of a retail store may start a conversation with a data scientist with a statement such as:

"We want a predictive model to identify our best customers."

So the first question to ask is:

"What do you mean by best?"

To which the sales director responds:

"Those customers who will make the biggest financial contribution to our business."

OK, that seems reasonable, but does "financial contribution" relate to gross sales or net profit? Are we talking about contribution per store visit, per click, or per unit time (week/month/year)? Are we looking at individual or household contribution when we talk about "customers"? and the list goes on. A data scientist needs to tease out a precise definition of what the business wants, and then express this in a way that can be represented by the scores generated by the model that they build.

In this example, it may be that after some discussion with the marketing director it's agreed that the model will be designed to predict the total gross spend of individuals per quarter year. Quarterly gross spend is selected because it aligns with the organization's reporting period and total revenue (sum of spending) is the key performance indicator for the sales director.

Individual rather than household spend is chosen because it's agreed that although household spend would theoretically be better, the organization's customer databases are structured at an individual not household level. It would not be possible to deploy a model based on household spend with the organization's current IT infrastructure. Could the IT be upgraded to provide a household view? No, certainly not as part of this project because the business has not allocated any budget for IT changes this year.

Given this information, the data scientist should determine that this is a regression type problem to predict the amount each individual customer will spend over a three month forecast horizon.

In parallel to determining how to express the business objective quantitatively, a data scientist needs to undertake exploratory analysis to understand the organization's data and IT assets, how they work, and how they interact with each other and the wider business. This includes:

- What databases does the organization have?

- What is the purpose of each database and what business processes make use of them?

- What do the databases contain? i.e. what data items and the format of those data items. For example, if it's numeric or textual data.

- How is each database updated and maintained? Most organizations have a mix of "real time" customer databases that are updated as soon as something changes, and batch databases which are updated less frequently; e.g. overnight or at month end.

- What decision-making systems are already in place? Will the model be implemented within an existing system or will new functionality be required?

- What data does the organization currently use for decision-making purposes? Even if this data feeds an antiquated manual process, it's likely that this data will be extremely valuable for machine learning purposes because the organization has already identified it as useful.

In a perfect world, every organization would have comprehensive documentation (metadata) that provides an inventory of its data assets. This is in terms of the types of data it holds, how that data is formatted, where it comes from and how it's used. However, in practice this sort of information is often patchy, incorrect or out of date. A lot of useful information is held in the heads of business users, who use it on a regular basis as part of their day jobs. There may be a data item called "Customer demographics 3" which contains letters A, B,…, G. What on earth does that mean? It's not documented anywhere, but Claire in Operations knows that it matches the income grades they use. "A" means an annual income of under $20,000, "B" $20-35,000 and so on.

Many organizations also maintain data that they no longer understand. Yet, they are afraid to purge it on the off chance it's something vital that a business-critical process relies upon. Potential new data sources, both internal and external, should also be examined during the exploratory analysis phase as these may enhance the predictive ability of any models which are developed.

Overall, a great deal of effort is required to explore the universe from which data can be gathered and to decide what can potentially be used and what cannot.

Once a data scientist has a good understanding of what data an organization has and how it is structured, then they can move to Stage 3 and think about creating the development sample that is going to be used in the machine learning process.

A very naïve approach to building predictive models is simply to throw every piece of information that an organization has into the machine learning process. In practice, much data is out-of-date, unstable or otherwise inappropriate. It should therefore be excluded from the development sample in case it degrades the performance of the machine learning process.

Some typical reasons to exclude data from the machine learning process are:

- **Out-of-date data.** If the data is no longer relevant to today's world then don't consider it. Data about how people used their cell phones in the time before smartphones existed isn't going to be very useful in telling you about smartphone usage today.

- **Not representative of the target population.** The development sample should only contain cases that mirror the population the model is going to be applied to. If a revenue model is being developed exclusively for online customers, then you should exclude in-store transactions if spending patterns are different for these two channels. Likewise, if you are developing a speech recognition system from sound samples, all samples should be speech related. If you have examples of barking dogs or traffic noise, then these need to be removed.

- **Stability of data.** Will the data used in the machine learning process be available when the model is applied? If a data item is not available at the point of implementation, then it should be excluded.

- **Legal and ethical reasons.** Do you want to use sensitive personal data such as race, gender and sexual orientation? This type of data can be very predictive, but it may be illegal to use it. If it is legal, then the use of such data may create reputational risk if it becomes known that you treat certain groups differently than others. If a discount strategy based on model scores results in you only offering discounts to straight men – that's going to be controversial.

- **Deterministic cases.** If you have customers which you know with certainty how you are going to treat them, then you don't need a predictive model for this. Including them in the development sample will only weaken the power of the model, as measured on the remainder of the population[47].

- **Inexplicability.** A fundamental principle of machine learning is that you should be very cautious about building models using data which you don't fully understand. This is particularly true for models that are subject to industry regulation or are strategically important to an organization's success. If a data scientist presents you with a model using data that they can't explain, then that's a risk that you should be concerned about.

If an organization has huge databases, then this may be problematic in terms of the computer resources required to analyze them as part of the machine learning process. It's not unusual for only a sample; say 1:10 or 1:100 cases to be selected for inclusion in the development sample.

"Big Data Purists" may argue that you should analyze all available data because failing to do so may result in subtle patterns being missed, and hence sub-optimal models being created. In one sense they are right. If you take a sample rather than using the full population the resulting model will not be as accurate. However, it's very much a case of diminishing returns. For almost all practical business problems, the benefits of taking more than a few tens of thousands of cases is marginal. If you sample in an appropriate way[48], then you'll get 99% of the benefit from a model developed using 100,000 cases compared to one developed using 10 million. To put it another way, just because you have huge amounts of data does not necessarily mean that you need to invest in specialist hardware/software to be able to apply machine learning – you just need to be smart in how you do it and focus on the data that really matters.

The fourth stage of the process is data preparation. This is required because the raw data may be badly formatted, contain errors or not provide the best possible representation of the data; i.e. a different representation will make it easier for the machine learning process to find the important patterns in the data. There are four main tasks that occur during data preparation:

1. **Creation of new data.** Age is more predictive than Date of Birth for most types of problem. Therefore, age may need to be calculated if only Date of Birth is available. If you have data about credit card transactions, it's best to create summary variables representing average spend per transaction, number of transactions last month, time since last transaction and so on.

2. **Data cleaning.** Data may be missing or incorrect. A key purpose of data preparation is to identify where this type of data exists, and to either remove it (an exclusion) or reformat it; i.e. recode all incorrect/missing data with a standard value. If dates of birth used to calculate age are in the future or impossibly far in the past, you may want to define a default value of say '-1' for age, to represent these cases.

3. **Consolidation**. It's good practice to represent similar data in a similar way. If you have a data item called Property Type, where the values "D", "Det" and "DH" all mean the same thing; i.e. "Detached House", then these should be consolidated into a single value that is used to represent all cases of Detached House.

4. **Conversion to numeric.** Machine learning algorithms like numeric data. "Yes"/"No"/"Maybe" would be converted in to 0/1/2 flags instead. For complex text or speech such as a Twitter feed, then one approach is to include flags to indicate if certain key words feature or not, or to generate counts of the number of times certain words appear.

Once a suitable data sample has been prepared then it's time for data pre-processing and preliminary variable selection (Stage 5 of Figure 12). With data pre-processing, one is putting the data into a format that is going to be most amenable to the chosen machine learning algorithm.

Pre-processing usually involves two processes: standardization and transformation. Standardization processes scale data so that everything has similar values. If you have two data items such as gross annual income in dollars and height in meters then one approach to standardization is to subtract the respective average and then divide by the range of values (or some other measure[49]). In this way, both will be centered on zero and have broadly similar ranges.

If we are talking about applying machine learning to something like an object recognition system, then similar standardization procedures are applied to the images that form the development sample. In object recognition, the development data is derived from the set of pixels in each image. Data about the color and intensity of each pixel provides the inputs to the machine learning process. Images in the development sample may have been taken under different lighting conditions. Therefore, the intensity of the pixels in each image are adjusted (standardized) to the average pixel intensity across all images.

Variable selection (variable reduction) is about deciding what data items to throw away and what should be retained and presented to the machine learning algorithm. The main reason for doing this is that even though today's computers are incredibly powerful, there is often too much data to process it in realistic time. Often, there will be thousands or even millions of individual data items that have been created during data preparation and data pre-processing. In most cases, only a handful of these actually prove to be materially important for generating accurate predictions.

Variable selection is usually a relatively quick and simple process. Various statistical tests are performed to determine how well correlated each piece of observation data is with the outcome being predicted. Data items are only retained if there is proven correlation. Typically, no more than between 1% and 10% of data items are retained following this process. There are also methods such as **Principle Component Analysis (PCA)** which seek to transform a large set of initial data items into a smaller set of new ones. These new data items are the ones that are then used for model construction.

Step 6 of the process is model construction. This is often the most exciting part of the machine learning process for a data scientist. It's what data scientists tend to talk about most of the time, even though model construction represents only a few percent of the overall end-to-end process. During model construction the development data is presented to the machine learning software, the relevant algorithm(s) are run and a predictive model is produced at the end. This would typically look something like the scorecards, decision trees and neural networks that we've seen before in previous chapters.

Modern machine learning software is highly automated. A wide range of algorithms are available at the push of a button. Many also provide features that deal with data preparation, pre-processing and variable selection. Consequently, some would argue that you don't need a PhD in statistics or machine learning to be able to develop predictive models, and in one sense that's true. However, a little knowledge is a dangerous thing. If you don't have the relevant technical background then you may not prepare or pre-process the data appropriately. Likewise, there are usually a range of different options that can be chosen for a given algorithm and you need to know how each option can impact the solution that is delivered. Similarly, you may not be able to interpret the outputs from the software or know what actions you should take based on what those outputs are telling you.

Machine learning algorithms are just sets of rules and logic statements that are applied in a certain way to create a predictive model. Sometimes things go wrong. It's quite possible for the software to (correctly) report that the model that has been created is highly accurate when in fact the model is useless.

Consider a predictive model, developed using machine learning, which predicts if people will default on their mortgages. The model is going to be used to decide which mortgage applicants to advance funds to and which mortgage applicants should be refused credit. It's pretty important that this model works because billions of dollars will be at stake if money is lent to the wrong people.

The software reports that the model correctly predicts mortgage default with 97% accuracy. Is this a good model? A naïve (and incorrect) response is yes, of course it is – that's nearly 100% and you can't get better than that. Also, you would expect a rubbish model would get it right about 50% of the time; i.e. it's performance would be similar to random guessing. So, the model is much better than that, isn't it? Hold on there a minute, cowboy! Let's take a step back and have a look at the development sample. This contains historic information about mortgage applications and their subsequent repayment performance. Let's say that 98% of people repay their mortgages on time and 2% default. I can easily outperform the predictive model by simply saying that I predict all mortgages will be repaid. I'll only be wrong in the 2% of cases that default. The accuracy of my predictions is 98% Something must be wrong because my simple "accept everyone" rule[50] is more accurate than the one derived using an advanced machine learning algorithm! This is just one example of the sorts of thing that need consideration when assessing how good a predictive model is and if it has been constructed correctly.

Once a model has been built using the development sample, then work is required to assess the model's performance (Step 7). From a technical perspective, this primarily involves assessing the predictive accuracy of the model on different data samples. These should be completely independent of the data used to build the model so as to provide a fair and unbiased view of how the model will perform when applied operationally to new cases. In particular, if the development sample was created a few months previously, then the model should be assessed using more recent data to ensure that it continues to perform as expected. A data scientist may report model performance as measured on the development sample, but they should base all of their final assessments of model performance on one or more independent validation samples.

Other validation activity may be more qualitative in nature, to check against any legal restrictions that may apply to how certain types of data are used and to ensure that the data used in the model will be available when the model is applied; i.e. if the model is going to be integrated into one of the organization's systems, then the data required to calculate models scores will need to be available within that system.

Machine learning is an iterative process. Often, many models are built using variants of different algorithms and/or different representations of the data before a final model is agreed upon.

Given more time and resource it's always possible to find another small improvement in predictive accuracy. However, in the real world time and resources are finite. Therefore, a decision needs to be made as to when to stop the machine learning process, review the models that have developed and decide which one to accept as your final model.

From a business perspective, assessment of the final model should be expressed in terms of key performance indicators and bottom line benefits. These should have been considered right at the start of the process. Consider an automated advice service that has been developed for a credit card provider to improve efficiency within their customer contact centers. The company developing the solution has decided to call this an "Autonomous Robotic Advisor" to make it sound like a cool and sexy modern AI type product.

The decision-making part of the system has been constructed using data from previously recorded customer service calls. A predictive model (a deep neural network in this case), has been developed from a development sample that contains several hundred thousand previous phone conversations with customers. These have been classified into the following types of enquiry (event):

1. Asking for the balance on their account.

2. Wanting a list of recent transactions.

3. Reporting a lost or stolen credit card.

4. Requesting to close their account.

5. Something else.

Events 1 to 4 are the most common types of customer enquiries, accounting for around 60% of customer calls, and are currently dealt with by human advisors. Given that the first four events require relatively simple standard responses, it should be possible to fully automate the customer service process for these types of enquiry.

If the query relates to something else (event 5) then the system will refer the call to a human to be dealt with. Likewise, if at the end of the automated response to events 1-4 the customer indicates that they are not happy with the response received, then they can still speak to a real person if they want to.

When a customer calls in, their speech is first pre-processed into a set of data items that provide the inputs to the machine learning process. These data items are predominately flags or counters representing specific words, phrases and sentences associated with certain types of customer enquiry.[51] The predictive model produced from the machine learning process then generates probabilities as to the likelihood that the customer's question falls into each of the five categories. Once the Robotic Advisor has identified what is most probably being asked, a suitable reply can be formulated. If the Robotic Advisor determines that the customer is most probably asking for their current balance, then the relevant information is retrieved from the company's account management system and an automated response is provided. "Your outstanding balance is $XXX".

When implementing the Robotic Advisor, what the call center manager will want to know are things like:

1. If we maintain the same customer services levels, then how many fewer staff will I need and hence, how much money will be saved?

2. If we employ the same number of staff as we do now, by how much will service levels improve? Staff should have more time for customers, given that the Robot Advisor will be dealing with a significant proportion of the calls received.

3. How often will the customer not get the right answer to their question if it's dealt with by the Robot Advisor? It's based on a predictive model. Therefore, it will get things wrong some of the time.

There will also be trade-offs between these outcomes. You may be able to use the Advisor to reduce staffing levels, improve service levels or a bit of both. If you want to ensure that the system only answers queries if it is almost certain to give the right response, then you will get far more referrals to human operators than if you are willing to accept a high error rate. If a threshold is set to only to respond to customers if the probability of the system giving the right answer is say, above 99%, you will get far more referrals to human underwriters than if you set the threshold at 80%. The issue then is one of customer service. If you set the threshold at 80%, then up to 20% of customers are going to be dissatisfied because the system will give them the wrong answer in 1 out of every 5 cases[52], as opposed to 1 in 100 cases.

To be able to answer questions like this and formulate appropriate decision rules (Stage 9), the data scientist will need to gather information about the operational nature of the organization. This is so that they are able to quantify the business benefits of their work. Otherwise, how can they justify the value of what they have done?

If it's all about saving cost or increasing profit (which it almost always is) then in this example, the data scientist would need to find out how long different calls types typically last and how much each call costs the company. This, combined with figures about the proportion of calls that will be automated and the costs of developing the system, will enable a cost-benefit analysis of the Robot Advisor project to be undertaken.

So far in this chapter we have focused on the process for applying machine learning. But how long is it going to take a data scientist to deliver a predictive model to you? That's very much a loaded question. Lots of solution suppliers will tell you that they can develop models for you in just a few minutes. "All you need to do is upload your data to our cloud-based AI solution and we'll give you answers in seconds!" That's sort of true, but you need to consider the context within which machine learning is being applied. To have results in minutes, you need to have all of your data nicely collected in one place. You need to be not too fussed about how the model's predictions are arrived at, how they are delivered or in what format.

If you have multiple complex databases which need to be brought together, have lots of messy data and it's important that the resulting model conforms with various legislation and business requirements, then that's a different story. It could be many weeks, months or even years before a suitable solution is arrived at.

11. Operationalizing Machine Learning

Some organizations have been using machine learning for decades. This is particularly true in the financial services industry and in the marketing departments of large consumer-facing organizations such as supermarkets chains and department stores. For the Silicon Valley brigade, which includes companies such as Amazon, Google and Facebook, machine learning is at the very heart of everything they do. These organizations have well-established IT infrastructures, systems and processes for applying machine learning and implementing the results. They do it day in, day out – it's just business as usual.

For organizations who are new to artificial intelligence and machine learning, building a predictive model for the first time and then operationalizing it as part of an automated decision-making system can be a difficult task. Sometimes, it can take several months before the required data is ready and the machine learning process can begin. However, gathering the right data and then applying the relevant machine learning algorithms, as discussed in the previous chapter, are often the easiest parts of a machine learning project. This is because, at the end of the day, a predictive model is nothing more than a set of equations captured in a spreadsheet, a word document or other software. Once the machine learning process is complete, the results need to be operationalized if they are going to be of use.

The main challenge, particularly for organizations which have not used machine learning before, is to accept the use of automated decision-making. They need to:

1. Put in place the infrastructure to allow predictive models to become a key part of the organization's operational decision-making capability.

2. Be comfortable with the decisions that are made on the basis of the model's predictions. This includes establishing governance procedures to ensure that model-based decisions are acted upon as intended, comply with legislation and that these decisions are not ignored or overridden by employees except in specific pre-agreed situations.

Perhaps the biggest mistake an organization can make is to assume that successful machine learning is: "All about the model" when they should be thinking about things from the perspective of: "It's all about the business."

Machine learning may be something that can add value to what an organization does, but then again it may not. A useful analogy is building a car engine. The engineers can spend a lot of time building a very powerful and efficient engine. However, that engine isn't going to provide any benefit unless someone has thought about the design of the car body, the engine mounting and so on, into which the engine will be placed. Without the rest of the car the engine is useless. The same applies to machine learning. Unless there is a business process to slot the model into, the model won't be of much use.

If an organization is going to successfully integrate machine learning into its business processes, then there are five core areas that need to be considered, in the following order:

1. **Problem.** What is machine learning going to be used for? There needs to be a clear problem that machine learning can help with.

2. **Culture.** Can the business be persuaded to accept automated decision-making without human experts being involved? From a managerial perspective, are resources; i.e. people and money,

available to enable predictive models to be integrated into the relevant business process?

3. **Implementation.** What system or process will be used to put the model into practice? How will scores be calculated? How will decisions made on the basis of those scores be acted upon by the relevant business function?

4. **Development Data**. Does sufficient data exist to enable predictive models to be constructed?

5. **Analytical capability**. Does the organization have the software tools and expertise required to analyze data, apply machine learning and build good quality, usable predictive models?

At first sight, the ordering of this list may seem somewhat counterintuitive. Why, for example, is model implementation listed before the analytics? Surely one builds a model first and then thinks about implementing it?

Machine learning is good for a lot of things, but it's not always the case that an automated machine learning based solution is what you need. Likewise, just because it's technically possible to predict something it doesn't mean that you should or that the predictions will prove valuable. Therefore, one needs to begin with problem specification and a plan about how to address it. Thought needs to be given to how you are going to use machine learning within an organization before you apply it and so on.

If machine learning is going to be the answer to the problem, then the two critical items which need to be established before anything else is done are:

1. What is the uncertain event/value/thing that you want to predict? This needs to be something very clear and explicit. It needs to be easily measurable and can be represented as a simple indicator for classification problems or as a numeric value for regression problems.

2. What decisions and actions will be taken about how to treat people, based on the predictions made by the model?

There is no point developing a predictive model to predict events that are certainly going to occur. Likewise, if people are going to continue to be treated in the same way, regardless of the score that they receive, then what use is the model? If existing customers are always going to be offered the same level of discount off their next purchase, then there is no point building a predictive model to identify repeat shoppers. A repeat shopper model will only be useful if a differential incentive strategy is offered, based on the scores generated by the model. For example, not offering a discount to those the model predicts almost certainly will buy again (high scores) and offering large discounts to those at the other end of the scale (low scores), to encourage them to shop again at the store.

Identifying the right problem is critical. One limitation of machine learning is that it is very specific. In tax collection for example, are we interested in identifying incorrect tax returns (classification problems – has the correct amount been paid or not) or maximizing total tax revenues (regression problem, amount collected)? Lots of people make small errors in their tax returns. Spotting these is helpful but won't increase the overall amount of tax collected by much. In fact, a lot of people accidentally overpay by small amounts. If your model identifies these cases then you may end up paying back some of the tax paid rather than collecting more!

Tax authorities are resource constrained. If you want to maximize tax take then you should focus only on the largest cases, where underpayments are very significant. Tax authorities simply don't have the manpower to follow up every little underpayment. Therefore, the problem needs to capture this requirement. For example, ignoring tax discrepancies of less than $1,000. In a similar vein, a model built to predict heart disease will probably not be very good at predicting dementia and vice versa.

The second consideration when building predictive models is organizational culture, and the appetite for change within the business areas that will be impacted by the models. Existing working practices and resistance to new ways of working are often a barrier to the introduction of machine learning. This is particularly true when staff are expected to behave differently on the basis of what the model tells them; i.e. machine learning is going to change the way people do their jobs, and in some cases, it will result in job losses and/or a devaluation of their skills.

As a rule, experts in a field don't tend to trust predictive models to be as good as they are at predicting outcomes. What this means is that an expert will often override decisions made on the basis of a predictive model if they are given the opportunity to do so - in effect negating any benefits that the model would have delivered.

Whether overriding is going to be a problem or not often rests on whether the predictive model is implemented in an active or passive way:

- **Active Models.** The predictions (scores) generated by a model are acted upon automatically. No human involvement is required for actions to be carried out.

- **Passive Models.** The model scores are used to generate cases that are passed on to people, who then decide how to deal with them; i.e. nothing happens until someone does something with the cases generated by the analytics process.

A situation where active models are used is in debt collection. Predictive models are used to prioritize debtors on the basis of which ones are most likely to repay what they owe. The prioritized lists are loaded into a dialer which then automatically calls people in list order.

When contact is made with a debtor, the call is transferred to a human debt collector who tries to persuade the debtor to repay what they owe. The debt collectors themselves aren't concerned with the order in which cases are presented to them. They simply process each case that they receive. Consequently, once the model has been implemented no further human input is required to decide on the ordering of the call list maintained in the dialer.

An example of a passive model on the other hand, is one that has been designed to rank job applicants in order of their suitability for a particular role. The model may be very good at picking out the most promising prospects, but a human interviewer is still required to meet the candidates and make the final decision about a job offer. If the interviewer takes a dislike to a candidate for whatever reason, then they won't offer the candidate the job, regardless of how good they would actually be at doing it.

Passive models are the most problematic. This is because in many organizations those at the front line have the ability to change or alter decisions that were made centrally. In the recruitment example, the power of the model is increasingly diminished the more the interviewers decide to override model based decision with their own. Also, human assessors often display bias (consciously or unconsciously) that disadvantages good candidates based on some unfound prejudice or stereotype, resulting in many good candidates having their job applications turned down.

Another example that I came across was in tax collection. A central function was responsible for identifying potentially fraudulent tax returns, and these cases were then passed on to locally based tax inspectors to carryout detailed investigations. The tax inspectors had the power to reject cases that they felt weren't suitable or which were unlikely to yield much additional tax.

When the central function implemented a predictive model to identify cases that were highly likely to be fraudulent, the number of cases rejected by the tax inspectors rose dramatically. This wasn't because the cases generated by the model weren't fraudulent. It was because the model was too good at identifying fraudulent activity due to very subtle signs in the data.

When a case arrived on a tax inspector's desk, the inspector was unable to establish exactly what was fishy about it. They didn't know how to go about beginning an investigation and consequently they rejected it. Likewise, the model often selected cases that were very complex or where it would be very difficult to collect the unpaid tax even though fraud had clearly occurred.[53] These types of cases also had a tendency to be rejected.

Active models are much easier to implement successfully than passive models. This is because people don't have the opportunity to override model based decisions. For example, once a decision has been made to post a customer a discount voucher, the process of dispatching the voucher, with a covering note, is automatic. No one is second guessing the system and giving vouchers to customer that they believe don't want them or won't use them. This is one reason why machine learning has been such as success for things like target marketing, credit granting and insurance pricing, yet is less well utilized in areas such as health care, human resources, policing and education.

The third item in the checklist, after problem definition and culture, is implementation. As discussed earlier, machine learning is all about making faster, better and cheaper decisions. Predictive models can be implemented manually in a spreadsheet and scores can even be calculated using a pen and paper, but in most cases predictive models are embedded within an automated decision-making system. The system uses the model to make predictions about how people will behave, and then takes decisions about how to treat people based on those predictions; e.g. the decision to grant a loan if the score is high enough.

By automating the decision-making process, individually tailored strategies for dealing with millions of people can be enacted in just a few seconds. What this means in practice is that organizations can update their predictions about people on a very frequent basis: monthly, daily, or even in real time, whenever a new piece of information about an individual is obtained.

Far more predictive models get developed than are ever implemented operationally. I've lost count of the number of organizations I've worked with where everyone gets really excited about the model building process but then neglects to think about how they are going to put the model to use once it's been built. Unless the infrastructure for using predictive models is already well established, the implementation of a predictive model is often a lengthier and more time consuming process than getting the model built in the first place. The most popular software packages for machine learning (R and Python) won't automatically deploy the models into an operational system for you. Model implementation needs to be considered, a budget approved and planning begun long before the data scientists are let loose to start gathering data and building models[54]

Generally, there are two ways that organizations implement models. The first approach is to treat implementation as an IT project. A programmer is employed to "code up" the model within an organization's IT system so that the required scores and decision rules are calculated when and where they are needed. This is a common approach, but it's amazing how often models are incorrectly coded due to simple errors – such as giving someone 100 points instead of 10, or plus 15 points instead of minus 15 points in a scorecard. There are also prioritization issues to contend with. It's not unusual for model implementation to take months or even years, due to other tasks taking priority. It's also the case that following model implementation, trying to get changes to a model or the associated decision rules is a nightmare. This is because every change has to go back into the IT work queue for prioritization.

The second approach to model implementation is via specialist software that provides an interface between the machine learning software used to build the model and the operational environment where the model is going to be deployed. When the model is complete the data scientist simply hits the "upload" button in the software, which then deploys the model (and associated decision rules) to the operational environment.

The main benefit of this approach is that, in theory, models can be implemented almost as soon as they are built. Importantly, it's the data scientists and business users who control the implementation of the model and associated cut-off (decision) rules. Little or no input is required from the IT department. This avoids lengthy delays that might otherwise arise if model implementation were to be placed in the IT work queue.

The penultimate consideration before the analytics process can begin is data. Data is the primary ingredient in the analytics process. It's essential. Without data, and the right type of data, useful models cannot be constructed or deployed. Therefore, before any thought is given to running machine learning algorithms to build a predictive model, due consideration needs to be given to the data that is going to be used. In particular:

- **Development sample data.** As discussed in Chapter 5, a reasonably sized sample of data is required. This sample needs to include both historic observation data and more recent outcome data.

- **Operational availability.** Any data that features in the resulting model must be available when the model comes to be implemented.

- **Operational stability.** If the relationships in the data change, then a model based on that data will lose some of its predictive ability. Therefore, a new model will be required.

It's important to remember that the development sample used to build a predictive model is historic, but the predictive model that results is going to be deployed in the future. In the months or years since the development sample data was recorded there may have been significant changes to the way the organization gathers and stores data. If certain data items are not going to be available going forward, then those data items should not be used to build the model. This is because it will not be possible to put the model into production. The data needed by the model simply won't be available.

It may be that in the past net income was obtained from customers and this is what is contained in the development sample data. However, because net income is sometimes difficult for customers to remember, the marketing department decided that it would be more customer friendly to switch to capturing gross income instead. If a predictive model was built using net income, it would not be possible to implement the model correctly because net income would no longer be available following the change to the way income is captured[55].

Once the problem has been specified, and cultural, implementation and data issues have been addressed, then one can start to think about the analytical process of building the model. This is where the specialist skills of a data scientist come into their own.

When it comes to the technical aspects of building a predictive model, a data scientist needs to consider a range of issues, as discussed in the previous chapter. Generating the most predictive model possible is obviously one concern, but the complexity, explicability and transparency of the resulting solution also need to be considered in light of organizational and regulatory requirements.

If we take banking as a case in point, the predictive models used to generate estimates of the capital that banks must hold in reserve are subject to extreme scrutiny by financial regulators. The model builder must fully describe the analytical process that was applied to construct the model, explain exactly how the model generates its predictions, and then highlight any material weaknesses that the model may have. "Black box" solutions that simply spit out very accurate, but inexplicable predictions will not pass muster. Likewise, in areas such as tax collection, medical diagnosis and criminal investigation, subject matter experts often favor models that they can understand.

However, if we shift the emphasis to models that are used in target marketing, those used to select matches on dating sites, or form part of a language translation system, then the user has far less interest in understanding the underlying model logic. Predictive accuracy is the overriding consideration. If it works it works, and that's all that matters.

Before choosing which type of model to develop and what algorithm to apply, a data scientist should have consulted with the business. They should have asked the right questions to make sure that they deliver a model that is predictive, conforms to regulatory requirements and takes into account any other issues or constraints that the business has highlighted.

Once the analytical process is complete and a predictive model is available, then it can be transferred to the area where it will be implemented. Assuming model implementation was given due consideration at the right point in the project, then this should be a relatively smooth process. This is because the necessary software and IT should already have been deployed, and operational staff briefed about how things will change when the model comes on-line.

Implementing an automated decision-making process using models developed via machine learning is a great achievement, particularly if it's something new for the organization in question. However, that's not the end of the process. Once a model goes live, the decision-making process needs to be the subject of regular review to assess how well the model is predicting and to ensure that the right cut-offs and decision rules continue to be applied.

Monitoring is required because a model's predictive accuracy tends to decline over time due to changes in the underlying relationships between the data used to construct the model and the outcome being predicted. Monitoring usually involves producing a set of reports showing how accurate the predictions made by the model proved to be. When model accuracy begins to fall, then that indicates that it's time for a new model to be developed.

Fall in predictive accuracy as models age is the primary reason why models need to be redeveloped, but predictive models are also redeveloped for other reasons. Sometimes there are legal or regulatory changes that mean that certain data items in a model can no longer be used. Likewise, new data sources become available, holding out the promise that more accurate models with greater predictive power can be constructed.

Another reason for carrying out regular model monitoring is to assess how the model based decisions affect different groups within the population. If the marketing department of a bank wants to target people with a certain geo-demographic profile with a new type of credit card, then it's important for the bank to understand how its credit scoring models treats those types of people. The last thing the bank wants to do is undertake a huge marketing campaign for new customers and then see all those that apply for the new card being declined.

Likewise, if a model is involved in making important life changing decisions about people, then it's prudent to monitor the model to ensure that any biases it displays are acceptable. If an HR department is using a model to screen job applicants and it is found to be rejecting a higher than average proportion of people from ethnic minorities or women, then that will need to be investigated and remedial action taken if necessary.

12. The Relationship Between Big Data and Machine Learning

Since about 2010, "Big Data" has become the ubiquitous term used to describe all the data that is generated by people from their smartphones, web browsing history, social media and purchasing behavior, together with any other information that organizations hold about them[56].

Why is Big Data different to any other type of data? In one sense there isn't a difference; it's all just zeros and ones at the end of the day. However, the term "Big Data" tends to be applied to large collections of different types of data which are often volatile and changeable, and where one would struggle to analyze it using traditional computer hardware and software.

It's also the case that Big Data often incorporates certain types of data that were not widely used for customer analysis until relatively recently. In particular, Big Data includes:

- **Text.** What people write and say can be analyzed to identify what they are talking about and the sentiments being expressed. If a product is being discussed in a positive or negative context, this is likely to be predictive of whether someone goes on to buy that product.

- **Images.** This covers photos and video, as well as medical imaging. One application of machine learning is to use features identified in scans and x-rays to predict the likelihood that someone has a specific disease.

- **(Social) network data.** This is information about people's connections and who they know. Network data includes the number and type of connections that people have, as well as data about connected individuals. If all your friends are sci-fi geeks, that's probably a good indication that you might be one too.

- **Geospatial.** Information about people's location and movements, provided by smartphones, in car GPS systems and other mobile devices.

- **Biometrics**. Data about blood pressure, heart rate and so on, collected from fit bands, smart watches and so on.

- **Product (machine) generated**. Everyday devices from televisions to coffee makers are being designed to share information between themselves and over the internet. These days your heating, kettle, washing machine and so on, can all be controlled via your smartphone. The **"Internet of Things"** (IoT) concept is still developing but may eventually provide lots of data that can be used to infer people's behavior using machine learning.

In the "good old days" back in the 1990s smart devices didn't exist. Few people even had a cell phone back then and the internet was still in its infancy. Very little electronic data about people or their activities existed. What there was, was usually limited to a few geo-demographics such as address, age, income, gender and so on. This may then have been supplemented by data supplied from a direct marketing company or a credit reference agency if financial services products were involved (e.g. arrears status on loans and credit cards). Supermarkets had no idea what individual customers bought each week, insurance companies didn't know how people drove and health services held most of their patient records in paper files.

Life for a data scientist back then was pretty straightforward[57] because all of this (very limited) electronic data was usually held in a nice neat format of rows and columns (like one would find in a spreadsheet). The data was also relatively static. It was usually only updated very infrequently and at regular intervals– typically at month or year end.

In today's world, data is being updated much more frequently, often in real time. In addition, a lot more of it is "free form" unstructured data such as speech, e-mails, tweets, blogs, pictures and so on.

Another factor is that much of this data is often generated independently of the organization that wants to use it. This is problematic for many reasons. One is that if data is captured or generated by an organization itself, then they can control how that data is formatted. They can also put checks and controls in place to ensure that the data is accurate and complete. However, if data is being generated by external sources then there are no guarantees that the data is correct.

Externally sourced data is often "Messy." It requires a significant amount of work to tidy it up and to get it in to a useable format. In addition, there may be concerns over the stability and ongoing availability of that data, which presents a business risk if it becomes part of an organization's core analytical and decision-making capability.

What this means is that traditional computer architectures (hardware and software) that organizations use for things like processing sales transactions, maintaining customer account records and invoicing, are not well suited to storing and analyzing all of the new and different types of data that are now available. Consequently, over the last few years a whole host of new and interesting hardware and software solutions have been developed to deal with these new types of data.

In particular, modern Big Data computer systems are very good at:

- **Storing massive amounts of data.** Traditional databases are limited in the amount of data that they can hold at reasonable cost. New ways of storing data has allowed an almost limitless expansion in cheap storage capacity.

- **Data cleaning and formatting**. Diverse and messy data needs to be transformed into a standard format before it can be used for machine learning, management reporting or other data related tasks[58].

- **Processing data very quickly**. Big Data is not just about there being more data. It needs to be processed and analyzed quickly to be of greatest use.

The issue with traditional computer systems wasn't that there was any theoretically barrier to them undertaking the processing required to utilize Big Data, but in practice they were too slow, too cumbersome and too expensive to do so.

New data storage and processing paradigms, such as **Hadoop/MapReduce,** have enabled tasks which would have taken weeks or months to process to be undertaken in just a few hours and at a fraction of the cost of more traditional data processing approaches. The way that Hadoop does this is to store massive data sets across large networks (clusters) of cheap desktop computers, such as the ones you might have in your office or at home.

MapReduce is one example of a programing language that shares data processing tasks across a computer network, such as a Hadoop cluster. Each computer in the cluster is tasked to independently processes the data it holds. The results from each individual computer are then brought back together and combined to deliver a final answer.

Consider a company using Hadoop to store details of all of its billions of customer transactions across a network of several hundred computers. To summarize information about the transactions, such as summing up the financial value of all transactions that took place in the previous financial year, MapReduce would task each individual computer to sum up the details of the transactions it holds. Each computer then feeds its results back to a single controlling computer, which adds up the individual results to get the final number.

In theory, tens of thousands of PCs can be connected together to deliver massive computational capabilities which are comparable to the largest supercomputers in existence. If you need more processing power, then all you need to do is just buy a few more standard desktop PCs and hook them into the network.

Hadoop is available as a set of free (open source) programming tools and is used by many companies as part of their Big Data solutions. Many solutions suppliers have also taken the core Hadoop software and developed their own set of interfaces and supporting tools to provide tailored product offerings. Examples include Cloudera, Hitachi Vantara, IBM, Microsoft, SAP and Teradata, to name but a few.

Data (whether "Big" or "Small") has no intrinsic value in itself. A big mistake that an organization can make is to think that if they invest in a mass storage system such as Hadoop and collect every scrap of data they can about people, then that's going to add a lot of value to their business. However, all that data has to be worked into something useful if it's going to be of benefit. Machine learning is the key tool that does that. The data needs to be processed to identify significant features and relationships in the data, and to produce predictive models that tell you something about people's behavior based on what has happened before in the past.

A good way to think about the relationship between Big Data and machine learning is that the data is the raw material that feeds the machine learning process. The tangible benefit to a business is derived from the predictive model(s), customer clustering or other analytical outputs that are delivered at the end of the process, not the data itself.

Artificial intelligence, machine learning and Big Data, are therefore often talked about in the same breath, but it's not a symmetrical relationship. You need machine learning to get the best out of Big Data, but you don't need Big Data to be able use machine learning effectively. If you have a just few items of information about a few hundred people, then that's enough to start to apply machine learning to do things such as building models and making predictions, applying clustering to customers and undertaking other types of data analysis.

The more and better data that you have, the better your machine learning solutions will be, but having gigabytes or terabytes of data is not a prerequisite for practical machine learning.

13. Ethics, Law and the GDPR

The use of machine learning and predictive models raises some interesting ethical questions. This is especially true when they are used to create automated decision-making systems that decide how people will be treated without any human involvement in the decision-making process.

As automated decision-making systems become ever more prevalent across almost every aspect of our lives, then what we are saying is that we are no longer in control. Those once in positions of authority, whether it's a bank manager deciding who to lend to or a doctor deciding who to treat, have ceded control to the computers.

Is this a problem? If one could say categorically that the result would always be better outcomes for individuals then that would be acceptable to many people. However, it's important to appreciate that in many, and possibly most, situations organizations are using machine learning for their own benefit. They are striving to achieve their own objectives (i.e. maximize profit) not yours. Whether or not the resulting outcomes benefit the people who are the subject of those decisions is not their primary concern.

The implication is that as a society we need to be comfortable with the way that predictive models are being developed and deployed and that this aligns with our sense of what is right and proper. Appropriate checks and balances need to be put in place to prevent misuse of decision-making systems that rely on machine learning.

One problem is that what constitutes "ethical use" is not always clear cut. There are a range of views and opinions as to what is or isn't ethical when it comes to data and analytics. Therefore, what checks and controls are required is somewhat debatable.

One argument is that if a predictive model generates more accurate predictions than a human expert and implementing that model results faster and more efficient decision-making, then using that model is obviously the right thing to do. However, it's important to realize that the ends do not always justify the means. How one gets to a decision and what is deemed acceptable by wider society is also important.

Let's start by thinking about the data that is used to make predictions about peoples' behavior. Do you think it is acceptable to use information about someone's gender, age, religion, marital status, sexual orientation or race when deciding how someone is dealt with? i.e. should this type of data be allowed to feature in a predictive model?

To be fair, this is something of a trick question. The answer will be influenced by the type of decision being made. If we are talking about diagnosis or treatment of a medical condition, then most people would probably not be too concerned with any of this type of data being used if it leads to better outcomes for individuals. The fact that age and gender, for example, were predictive in the heart disease model (Figure 2) is not an issue. However, if we are talking about deciding who to hire or fire on the basis of things like gender or marital status, or charging people more for products and services because of their religion, then things are less clear.

From a purely statistical perspective, things like marital status, gender and age may indeed be correlated with things such as how well people perform in their jobs (And hence who to hire or fire). However, from a societal perspective, allowing a predictive model to drive decisions based on this type of data is ethically questionable and is illegal in many jurisdictions.

A very simple and simplistic solution to problems like this is to make sure that certain data items are prevented from featuring in some types of predictive model to ensure legal compliance. The algorithm that generates a predictive model is directed to exclude data such as gender, race and marital status from the machine learning process. That's fine, but just because a predictive model doesn't use certain data items directly doesn't mean that the model does not display unacceptable bias.

A great example of this is gender discrimination in insurance. It's a well-established fact that women present a lower risk than men for many types of insurance. However, in all countries that are members of the EU it is illegal to set insurance premiums on the basis of gender. Therefore, insurers don't use gender in the claim prediction models that they use to set premiums. However, there are other variables that often act as a proxy for gender. Income is one such data item. Why? Because there is gender bias in income distributions. Women on average earn less than men even when they are doing the same job and where wage discrimination on the grounds of gender is illegal. If a predictive model uses income as a predictor variable there is an indirect effect which means that women will be treated differently to men. As a consequence, a predictive model may have to be designed to be sub-optimal in terms of predictive ability. This is to ensure that, all other things being equal, it generates the same predictions for men and women with the same characteristics and hence, complies with the law.

Predictive models should conform with relevant legal and regulatory requirements – such as not displaying gender bias. However, that's not the end of the story. A very easy mistake to make is to think that if it's legal then it must also be ethical. Sure, there is some overlap between what's ethical and what's legal, but they are not the same thing. Good laws often seek to define behavior which society deems unacceptable; i.e. unethical, but at best, laws are generalizations of ethical behavior and are usually retrospective in nature.

Laws also tend to address problems that occurred in the past. They don't usually consider new situations before they arise. This means that there are always situations that are not covered by specific laws and there are almost always loopholes which exist to allow the unscrupulous to circumvent the law to get what they want. This is what people mean when they talk about the letter of the law as opposed to the spirit of the law.

OK - so an organization can be acting legally but not ethically, but why should a business that is concerned with maximizing the bottom line be concerned by that? One reason is pure self-interest.

There is a lot of evidence that if one is thinking about the long term, then adopting an ethical code of behavior delivers a real bottom line benefit.[59]

Another reason for thinking about ethical issues within the context of machine learning, and the data that predictive models use, is the risk of reputational damage. If the public decide that they don't like the way you operate, think that you treat people in an underhand way, or unfairly discriminate against certain groups, then those sentiments can devalue a brand immensely. Simply arguing that your predictive model is statistically valid and legally compliant isn't enough. If it comes to light that a model puts war veterans and children at the back of the queue for medical treatment (even though being a war veteran or a child are not explicit variables in the model) then you are going to be challenged about that – even if the decision-making process that uses the predictive model generates optimal patient outcomes measured across the population as a whole.

Another way to think about this is that ethical considerations should drive a number of constraints within decision-making systems, which need to be given appropriate consideration when the system is designed.

What should an organization do to incorporate an ethical perspective into their use of machine learning and automated decision-making? Unfortunately, there is not a clear cut answer to this question. One problem is the subjective nature of ethics. It's very much a personal thing. Two people may hold opposing, but equally valid opinions as to what constitutes acceptable behavior. Likewise, different legislative regimes approach personal data and how organization can use it in very different ways.

In the USA, the starting point when it comes to personal data and its use within automated decision-making systems is very much along utilitarian lines. Personal data is there to be harvested and used to maximize organizational goals e.g. maximize profit or minimize cost. If there is a problem using a specific type of data or there is unacceptable bias against a specific group, then legislation is enacted to address that particular concern.

This is very different to the approach adopted by countries within the European Union (EU). EU citizens have control over who can hold their data and how it's used. If they don't want their data to be used for a given purpose, then that's their decision, even if it leads to sub-optimal outcomes.

These two different perspectives are one reason why US based companies such as Google and Facebook struggle to find common ground with regulators over how personal data can be gathered and used in EU countries.

Another issue is that ethical considerations are often problem and domain specific. What's acceptable in one situation is not acceptable in another. As we've already discussed, most people are probably OK with sensitive personal information such as their religion and sexual orientation, being used to diagnose a medical condition. However, using these same data items to decide who can or can't get a mortgage is a far more questionable proposition.

Given the complexity around these issues, it's good practice for the builders of automated decision-making systems to undertake an ethical risk assessment as part of the design phase of the project. Also, many organizations are now standing up ethics committees to contribute to the governance process. The ethics committee is engaged at key points in a machine learning project and will ask those difficult questions that need to be asked about how the system is going to affect people. The ethics committee then gives its opinion on whether they believe that such a process aligns with their organizations ethical position, and if not, to detail what modifications are required to achieve that. A very simple starting point in this process is just to ask the following question: "Would I like this type of decision-making to be applied to members of my family?[60]"

In assessing the ethical risk associated with an automated decision-making system, there are three main aspects to consider:

1. **Beneficiary.** Who is going to gain from the decision being made? The more the decision maker benefits at the expense of the individual, the greater the ethical risk that that decision represents. An employer deciding who to employ is making decisions purely for their own benefit. Jobs are not offered on the basis of the benefit they give to the employee.

2. **Data Immutability.** There are some characteristics people are born with. These can't change. If decisions are made on the basis of things such as age and ethnic origin, then that's far more controversial than data that results from people's lifestyle choices, which are more dynamic and changeable. For example, the music people like or what they watch on TV.

3. **Impact (significance).** What effect is a decision going to have? A life or death decision about cancer treatment is much more important than something trivial such as deciding whether or not to send someone a 10% discount voucher for frozen pizza.

Bringing these three considerations together, it's when high impact decisions are being made using immutable data, purely for the benefit of the decision maker that the greatest ethical risks arise. Great care needs to be taken to ensure that the decision-making system is fair, displays no unacceptable bias and hence, does not expose the decision maker to accusations of misbehavior. I'm not saying that an organization can't use high impact immutable data to further their own ends, but that they need to be careful and be ready to respond to any challenges about the way they use that data.

If an organization identifies that it is using predictive models to take what are potentially "High risk" ethical decisions, then what should it do? The answer is to take mitigating action as follows:

1. Try to identify at-risk groups. The way to do this is to produce separate score distribution reports for groups such as women, ethnic minorities, children and so on. It can then be seen if there is any bias in the resulting scores; i.e. which groups tend to get lower than average scores and will therefore be adversely treated compared to the wider population.

2. For those groups that score less well than the population average, constraints and override rules should be used to ensure that they are treated in a fair way. Likewise, different cut-offs may need to be set for at risk groups.

3. Continue to monitor the situation once the decision-making system goes live. Regularly review the score profile and decision rules for key groups. Cut-offs, constraints and overrides should then be fine-tuned as required.

To illustrate this approach, let's think about an employment scenario. Consider a predictive model which is used to decide who to hire. A high score from the model indicates that the person is likely to be successful in the role, a low score less so. A concern might be that older men or people with young children are treated unfairly (which would potentially be in breach of EU law if the model was being used in that region). This is not to say that there isn't evidence that older men or people with children perform worse in their roles and would be worse hires than other people, but that it would be socially unacceptable to treat these groups differently. An ethically questionable system would be one where there was a single predictive model and a single cut-off score was applied to decide who to hire.

A more robust approach, is to start by producing separate score distributions for older men and people with children. These are then compared against the score distribution for all potential hires. If necessary, separate cut-offs are then applied. This is to ensure that the proportion of people who are offered jobs in these two groups is the same as for the rest of the population.

Another similar approach, is to construct separate models for each group. One model is built for the general population, one for older people and another for people with young children. Separate cut-off rules are then applied to each model to ensure that a consistent and aligned decision-making strategy occurs.

So far in this chapter we have focused on developing an ethical framework for dealing with personal data and how it can be applied in a general setting; i.e. what we have discussed is universally applicable to a wide range of situations wherever in the world one resides. Thinking about these issues will help you deal with individuals in a morally appropriate way (meaning you can sleep easy at night). However, as noted earlier in this chapter, governments and regulatory authorities around the world are introducing much tighter legal and regulatory controls over how organizations gather, store and use personal data. Therefore, regardless of how ethical an organization believes it is, it also has to comply with all relevant laws and regulations in the regions within which it operates.

Laws around the use of personal data and its use in automated decision-making have existed in many countries for decades but differ widely in scope and application. Some countries have very detailed regulation relating to personal data, while others have none at all.

In the US, regulation is narrowly targeted at specific uses of personal data. The Equal Credit Opportunity Act 1974 (ECOA) requires lenders to explain why their automated credit scoring systems decline people for credit. The Health Insurance Portability and Accountability Act 1996 (HIPAA) provides safeguards around the use of people's health records. The Children's Online Privacy Protection Act (COPPA) relates to data about children under the age of 13 and so on. In the US there is no overarching legislation specifically around the gathering of personal data or how that data is used in automated decision-making processes.

For the 28 countries that comprise the European Union, which includes 4 of world's 10 biggest economies with a combined population of more than half a billion, it's a very different story. A much more comprehensive approach to the regulation of personal data and how it can be used has been adopted for many years. What can be argued is the most significant data protection legislation ever enacted anywhere in the world came into force in all EU countries on 25th May 2018. The General Data Protection Regulation (GDPR) places great responsibilities on organizations over how they gather, manage and process peoples' personal information.

The GDPR applies to all organizations operating in the EU, even if their base of operations is elsewhere. There is no opt out for the tech giants operating out of Silicon Valley if they do business in any EU member state.

It's been said that the law is an ass, but the GDPR will kick yours if you ignore it. Organizations that fail to comply with the GDPR are liable for fines of up to 4% of global *turnover* (not profit) for every breach of the regulation that occurs. Even if you don't live in the EU it's worth spending a bit of time to get under the skin of it because it highlights the direction of travel for data protection legislation in a number of other countries and jurisdictions.

The GDPR adopts a rights based approach. The foundation stone that underpins it is personal ownership of one's own data. It's an individual's right to decide who has access to their data and how it's used. Data about me is mine, it's part of who and what I am. You have no right to hold or use my data unless I give you permission to do so. To store my data or make decisions about me without my permission is illegal. I also have the right to change my mind. I can give you access to my data today, but if I no longer want you to use it, then you must stop doing so and delete what you know about me.

The legislation is also principle based. This means that it's not entirely prescriptive in terms of what you have to do to comply. The aim is to encourage compliance with the spirit of the law not just the letter of the law.

Another factor to bear in mind is that the focus of the GDPR is squarely on the individual. There is no consideration as to the costs that organizations incur to comply. At best, there is only very limited scope for a business to argue that it would be uneconomic or might cause them to go bust unless they process data in a certain way.

The GDPR covers a wide range of issues relating to personal data and applies to all automated decision-making and profiling applied to living individuals[61]. The four areas that are particularly relevant in a machine learning/AI context are:

1. Explicit consent needs be obtained from someone before their personal data can be gathered or used. The consent can't be inferred or be "consent by default."

2. It is not permitted to make decisions about people, using an automated decision-making process which has a legal or similarly *significant* impact upon them[62] unless they have given their consent that automated decision-making can be used for this purpose. This is additional to the consent to hold data. The primary exception to this is where automated processing is necessary to allow a legal contract to be enacted[63].

3. An individual has the right to be provided with an explanation as to how an automated decision has been arrived at and the *consequence of that decision*[64]. This aligns with the more general requirement in the GDPR for organizations to provide individuals with information necessary to ensure that fair and transparent processing of their data occurs[65].

4. Automated decision-making systems must not display *unfair* discrimination; i.e. treating people differently on the basis of their race, sexual orientation and so on.

To obtain explicit consent the right approvals need to be in place. If we are talking about making decisions about employees, suitable clauses need to be included in their employment contracts. For consumers, approvals need to be provided via people ticking relevant tick boxes or similar.

For item 2, the key word is *significant*. If a decision is going to have a noticeable impact on an individual, then that person has the right to demand that the decision is reviewed manually. The law is clear that this review needs to be fully independent and undertaken by someone empowered to make a different decision to the one made by the system. It can't just be a case of clerical staff rubber stamping the original decision.

What makes this item difficult to apply in practice is that there is no accepted definition of "significant." Perhaps most importantly, what may be insignificant for some people may be very significant for others, even if it's only a very small proportion of the people processed through the system[66]. It can't be taken for granted that certain types of decision-making don't significantly impact people – it's got to be on a case-by-case basis. Imagine a supermarket chain that decides it will apply a differential pricing strategy. Customers who it believes can't or won't shop elsewhere are charged 5% more for their groceries than more fickle customers who shop around. For most customers this won't be more than a slight inconvenience, but for those on the poverty line it may represent a very real impact on their quality of life. What this means practically is that it may be prudent to always begin from the position that all decisions are potentially significant decisions unless there is sufficient evidence to the contrary.

With regard to item 3 - the right for an explanation about how a decision was arrived at - this requires an understanding of how a predictive model has been used. For instance, why someone's insurance premiums are a certain amount or why they were declined for a loan. As a minimum, an organization would need to tell an individual making such an enquiry:

- Which data items are used in the decision-making process. For example: "when assessing your application for a new phone contract, we use information about your age, income and marital status, together with information about your credit history to make a decision."

- The source of those data items. This could be direct from the individual via an app or online form, information that is publicly available such as voter records or information they have given other organizations permission to share, such as social media platforms or credit reference agencies.

- Details of which data items contributed to the decision and in what way. In deciding whether or not to accept someone's application for a phone contract, one might say that decisions are based on a credit score. The score uses information about people's credit history, and the number and recency of missed payments negatively impact the score. The applicant missed two mortgage payments last year resulting in a low credit score. Therefore, their application for a new contract has been declined[67].

In some cases, it is possible that a full technical explanation may also be required as to all of the individual model parameters, although at the time of writing the exact circumstances under which this would be required are unclear. One might assume that it will only be required in relatively few specific cases that reach the courts, rather than being something that is provided whenever a customer makes an enquiry. However, it's pretty clear under GDPR that: "Complexity is no excuse for failing to provide information to the data subject.[68]" In the UK, the Information Commissioner's Office made the following comment with regard to model explicability[69]:

> "Big data organisations therefore need to exercise caution before relying on machine learning decisions that cannot be rationalised in human understandable terms. If an insurance company cannot work out the intricate nuances that cause their online application system to turn some people away but accept others (however reasonable those underlying reasons may be), how can it hope to explain this to the individuals affected?"

What this means is that there's a potential barrier to using deep learning and other complex "black box" types of model to make decisions about people, unless a suitable explanatory mechanism also exists. It is possible to develop such mechanisms but this will require additional time and cost to produce.

Another factor that needs to be borne in mind is that individuals can change their mind. They may have given their permission to use their data for certain purposes at one time but that permission can be withdrawn at a later date. Likewise, the "right to be forgotten" requires organizations to delete personal data if a person requests it. Hence a process to deal with the changes in consent and the deletion of personal data need to be in place.

Finally, there is the issue of discrimination. All decision-making systems (automated or manual) discriminate – that's the nature of what they do. The question is whether *unfair* discrimination occurs. The GDPR is clear that specific items such as race, sexual orientation and so on, must not normally be incorporated into automated decision-making systems. However, one must also be able to identify and correct for indirect bias as we have discussed previously in this

Chapter.

Take all these things together, and what it means in practice is that the good old "Wild West" days of machine learning and advanced analytics are pretty much over when it comes to personal data. The practice of just letting a data scientist knock up a "quick and dirty" predictive model for your business function to use is all but gone – in EU countries at least. Instead, organizations which are investing in Big Data and automated decision-making processes need to:

- Assess the risks and issues associated with machine learning and automated decision-making up-front. It's not an add-on at the end of a project.

- Not expect to do away with all human expertise entirely. There must be a suitably trained operational function that can process decisions manually when required.

- Have suitable governance and audit processes in place to manage and provide oversight of their decision-making systems. This includes developing approaches to identify and mitigate risks as they arise, as discussed previously.

From a project management perspective, the requirement for governance and manual intervention can have a significant impact on the costs of developing and maintaining automated decision-making systems. If you are considering using automation within your organization, then this additional overhead needs to be included within the cost-benefit case undertaken before the project begins.

In terms of operational usage, if you use predictive models to do things like deciding who you are going to fire, then you need to have people who can review the data used by the model and who can override the original decision if necessary. In fields such as insurance and credit granting, this means that you'll need to retain expert underwriters who can challenge the decisions made by the organization's automated underwriting systems. There also needs to be a process in place to deal with customer queries about automated decision-making and to supply relevant information to them as required by the legislation.

14. The Cutting Edge of Machine Learning

Machine learning is an exciting and evolving subject that is being driven by new developments in three main areas:

1. **Models and Algorithms.** New machine learning approaches are being developed all the time. One avenue of research is looking at new types of model. Another seeks to improve upon existing algorithms that produce scorecards, decision trees, neural networks and so on, in order to improve the predictive accuracy of these types of model.

2. **Data.** Predictive models and other AI applications are only as good as the data used to build them. More/better data leads to better solutions. This is one reason why "Big Data" and machine learning are so closely related.

3. **Systems and software.** Improvements to the systems used to develop and implement automated machine learning based solutions are important since the faster a solution can be deployed the sooner the benefits will be realized.

Let's start by discussing the models and algorithms side of machine learning. Scorecards, decision trees and neural networks are probably the most widely used types of predictive model in use today. However, if you talk to the young bucks in Silicon Valley, they will probably laugh and then tell you that these types of model are somewhat "vintage" – decision trees are *so* 1980s! There are so many better types of predictive model out there these days...

In one sense this is true. Scorecards, decision trees and neural

125

networks are certainly not new. It's also the case that on average, newer types of predictive model such as deep neural networks, support vector machines and ensembles, generate more accurate predictions, particularly in areas where complex types of decision-making are required.

Scorecards and decision trees were first used commercially in the 1950s and 1960s, in an age when a typical computer was the size of a large desk and had less than 1% of the computational abilities of a basic smartphone today. Therefore, these simple types of predictive model could be developed and implemented relatively easily. Computer power is much less of an issue these days, but simple models such as scorecards and decision trees remain very popular for the following reasons:

- **They are "White Box" in nature.** It's very easy to understand how a score and hence a prediction about someone is arrived at. Likewise, it's easy to see which data items contributed most significantly to the score, and which are less important.

- **They are easy to code.** Specialist software is not required to implement them. If resources are tight, then you can implement a scorecard or a decision tree as a small IT project without needing to purchase additional hardware/software, and without needing to employ very expensive data scientists.

- **They still produce pretty good predictions, if not the best.** Some predictive models are thousands of times more complex than a simple scorecard or decision tree. However, even the most advanced predictive models often provide no more than a few percent uplift over simple scorecards or decision trees, and sometimes none at all.

What I want to make clear is that the big win for organizations is to make the leap to using automated decision-making in the first place, based on machine learning. The incremental benefits from using the most advanced methods available are often more marginal. This is particularly true where the business problems are simple and can be expressed precisely and concisely, such as assessing default risk on a loan or how likely someone is to respond to a marketing campaign. It's the more complex and convoluted types of problem such as face recognition, language translation and autonomous driving which have benefited most from advanced forms of machine learning such as deep neural networks.

If your organization does not currently use machine learning, then developing some simple predictive models that can be integrated into your existing decision-making infrastructure will give you most of the benefits. The fancy cutting-edge stuff, which often requires specialist hardware and/or software, will provide greater benefits, but not a massive amount. Therefore, don't delay. The 80/20 rule applies. You'll get 80% of the benefits for 20% of the effort.

It's also the case that if you can't get a simple predictive model to work, then just using a more complex approach or buying some expensive hardware/software is unlikely to solve the underlying issues; i.e. the failure of a machine learning project is nearly always due to incorrect problem formulation, the underlying data or an organizational issue. The problem is unlikely to be due to the type of predictive model that has been developed.

OK. That's the argument for keeping faith with simple models such as scorecards and decision trees. However, if an organization is an established user of AI applications, developed using machine learning, and its predictive models are responsible for billions of dollars' worth of decisions each year, then there will be a drive to have the very best (most accurate) models possible – and with good reason. For a model that supports a billion dollars' worth of decision-making each year, then just a 0.1% uplift in performance equates to a $1m benefit. In this type of scenario, it would be perfectly justifiable to employ a team of data scientists full-time to constantly challenge and improve upon the models that the organization employs.

The most advanced forms of predictive models in use today are ensemble models, based on complex (deep) neural networks. With an ensemble, instead of having a single scorecard, decision tree or neural network model, hundreds or possibly thousands of different models are constructed. Each model is developed using a different data sample and/or a different algorithm to determine the model's parameters. Each model therefore, makes predictions in a slightly different way. The scores generated by each model will often be the same or very similar, but sometimes they will disagree with each other; i.e. some models will give certain cases very high scores, whereas other models will give the same cases much lower scores and vice versa.

Using an ensemble model is a bit like having decisions made by a committee of experts rather than by a single expert. The reasons why the committee approach is better than having a single expert is twofold:

1. If one of the experts has specialist knowledge, that the others don't have, then this can be brought into the decision-making process.

2. Some of the experts may, on occasion, make poor decisions. The other experts will use their collective knowledge to override (out vote) those cases.

Just like the committee, some of the models that form an ensemble will be particularly good at predicting the outcome of certain types of cases. If any of the models are weak in certain areas (generate poor predictions) then these are overridden by the others.

Once constructed, the way an ensemble works is pretty straightforward. The score from each model is used to make a decision. A final decision is then made by simple majority vote. If we return to the heart disease scorecard model discussed earlier, then imagine that instead of a single scorecard, a thousand different scorecards are constructed. The original decision rule was to invite someone for a check-up if they scored 521 or more. With the ensemble, if at least 501 of the individual models generate a score of 521 or more, then the decision is to invite.

How much better are ensembles than single models? Sometimes none! However, in my experience, it's not unusual for an ensemble to be around 5-10% better than a single model. If an insurance company found that using a decision tree resulted in a $40m reduction in claims over their previous manual process for the same amount of underwriting, then moving to an ensemble approach could reasonably be expected to provide an additional $2-4m benefit.

If all you are interested in is raw predictive accuracy, then ensembles are the way to go. If however, it's important for you to be able to explain how a model arrives at a given prediction, then you may want to think twice before going down the ensemble route because the solution will be much more complex and more difficult to understand than a single model approach.

Let's now move on to think about data. From reading the academic literature on machine learning, I would hazard a guess that 95% or more of it is about algorithms; i.e. very technical discussions about the cutting edge mathematical approaches that can squeeze a little bit more predictive accuracy from a given data set. In practice however, when it comes to improving the accuracy of predictive models, data is king.

Given a choice between a new algorithm for building a predictive model and having more/better data available, then data wins every time. To put it another way, very simple predictive models built using a large amount of high quality data almost always outperform more advanced approaches built using a smaller amount of lower quality data. If you really want to get more out of your predictive models, then improving the quality of the data used to build them and seeking out new and better data sources, should come at the top of your priority list.

In the early days of Big Data, when the cost of data storage fell very dramatically in a short period of time, there was very much a "store and analyze it all" data philosophy amongst the pioneers. The message was that every organization should be gathering and analyzing all the data it could. Back then, there was a lot of talk about needing to invest in mass storage systems such as Hadoop. This was to allow organizations to store all the data that they could lay their hands on in order to be able to produce the best predictive models possible and hence, gain a competitive advantage. However, the amount of data being generated has continued to increase year on year and shows no signs of slowing down. In fact, the volume of data is increasing at a far faster rate than the cost of data storage is falling.

This means that the benefit of having all available data to hand is to some extent offset by the costs of storing and analyzing all that data. As discussed previously, only a small fraction of all the data out there actually features in predictive models and is used to make predictions; i.e. once you know what types of data are predictive of how people are going to behave then you can discard most of the other data because you don't need it. Continuing to maintain huge databases of "low value" data is not a very efficient use of time and resource.

These days there are moves towards common data storage and aggregation – particularly when it comes to externally sourced data and data that is common across organizations. If people have ten apps on their phone supplied by ten different organizations, then it's very wasteful for each of those organizations to be gathering location and movement data themselves. It makes far more sense for one organization to manage the data, and then provide clients with the specific data items that are relevant to them.

If you look at companies such as Facebook, Google, Experian, Equifax and so forth, then this is exactly what they are doing. They undertake the hard work of collecting, formatting, preparing and summarizing data. They then package the useful bits and sell it on. In this way, individual organizations only acquire data that is genuinely useful to them. Consequently, they don't need to waste time and resources gathering huge amounts of data that they don't need.

The third driver of developments in machine learning is IT systems and software. As the volume of personal data has grown, and the frequency with which data changes has increased, so cycle times between model developments has reduced in many industries.

The traditional paradigm for developing and implementing predictive models is to separate these two parts of the process; i.e. develop your models first and then implement them. During the development phase a data scientist spends days, weeks or even months gathering data and carrying out the statistical analysis required to build the model. When that part of the process is complete there is a further exercise to code up the model within the production environment, test that the model works and then for it to be put into live operational use.

In many (and possibly most) industries this approach to predictive models is still applied and generally works pretty well, not least because after a model has been developed it has to pass internal and external audit, and then be subject to regulatory review before it can be put to use. Regardless of what the law says, having a robust model governance structure in place is important. This is because if your entire business relies on the correct decisions being made, and you get it wrong, then the impact on the bottom line can be very considerable indeed.

For the risk models used in banking and insurance to determine how much capital they need to hold in reserve[70], it can take a year or more between a predictive modelling project commencing and a model being implemented within the business. Every aspect of the model has to be fully documented and then a cycle of discussion, feedback and further analysis needs to occur before the regulator signs-off the model as fit for use. Banking regulators won't even deem to review a predictive model until it has undergone a complete review by independent experts. This can take as long or longer than the initial model building process.

In other areas however, such as internet marketing, things move much faster. Data, and the relationships in that data, are changing frequently, some of it in real time. If an organization wants to retain a competitive edge then it needs a much more rapid cycle of model development and implementation. Models are rebuilt on a daily or more frequent basis in response to constant changes in the data. This has led to the development of IT systems that closely integrate the data an organization holds, the analytical tools used to create predictive models and the systems that deploy them.

These "in-database" systems stream data to machine learning tools without needing to extract the data first, drastically reducing the time required to pull data samples together, build predictive models and then to deploy those models operationally.

Once an in-database system has been configured, models can be redeveloped and deployed automatically. In theory, a new and updated model can be constructed every time a new piece of data becomes available – the system learns from each new case it deals with. New models are developed and deployed on a minute by minute basis. Consequently, it becomes impossible for a data scientist to be involved in the detail of every model that is constructed. Instead, the data scientist's role is to be part of the team that designs the wider system. In particular, they have responsibility for understanding the data that feeds the system and how this maps to business problems that the system needs to create predictive models for.

After a system goes live the software provides a dashboard for the data scientist that reports on the status of the overall system. For example, how well models within the system are performing, how model performance changes over time, how the data that feeds the analytics process is changing and so on.

The data scientists themselves only become involved in the detail when something goes awry, or when some new feature needs to be incorporated into the system. If there is an unexpected dip in model performance the data scientist will need to investigate and find out why. They will then instigate remedial action to correct the problem and return the system to optimal operating conditions.

A similar approach is taken with self-learning devices and autonomous robots. Each time they undertake a task, they gather data about that event. The predictive models that drive their activities are automatically refined using the additional data available. In this way, as more and more data becomes available, so the accuracy of the underlying models improve.

A further focus of some of the newer machine learning software are intermediary tools which seek to provide a better interface between non-technical business users and the underlying data and algorithms required for machine learning.

The most advanced of these tools try to replace some of the tasks that would traditionally have been undertaken by data scientists. They can analyze and prepare data from different sources, apply a range of algorithms and present the results back to non-technical users in an easy-to-understand way without any formulas or equations. In particular, the software attempts to present results in a contextual way that makes business sense, rather than providing a more formal statistical perspective that data scientists are used to dealing with.

A prime example of this approach is the one taken by IBM with its Watson Analytics Software. The original version of Watson famously beat several human players in the general knowledge quiz show Jeopardy in the USA[71]. Watson has now evolved in to a commercial product. Behind the scenes, the software uses some very complex machine learning algorithms to extract information from a range of different data sources. The front end of the software is designed with managers and other business users in mind rather than data scientists.

The net result is that when presented with suitable data, new insights and understanding about the behavior of customers can be presented to business users within hours, or even minutes, without the need to involve technical specialists in the process.

15. When Can I Buy a Self-Driving Car?

Don't worry. I'm sure it won't be too long before you'll be able to pop down to your local dealer and buy one, and some would argue that you already can. However, if you mean a fully autonomous vehicle, that your visually impaired grandma can keep in her garage and be driven wherever she wants, then it might be a bit longer than all those media stories about self-driving cars might suggest.

To some, self-driving cars in the 21st century are what the moon landings were to the 20th century. It's a massive technical challenge, requiring billions of dollars of investment over a decade or more. Success will mark a significant milestone in our ability to replicate and exceed human abilities via artificial means. Just like the moon landings, there are a host of challenges to overcome and many steps along the way. Being able to fire a rocket into space or put a satellite into orbit is helpful, but it doesn't qualify you to put a man on the moon. That's a much grander challenge.

Recently, it dawned on me that a question that had been bugging me for quite some time was: "Where are all the self-driving cars?" No one seemed to mention them at the dealerships I visited recently when looking for a new car.

I remember reading years ago, in 2010 if not earlier, that self-driving cars were pretty much already here. One quote that comes to mind is: "It's crazy to imagine that we are going to keep driving cars like we do now – that in 10 to 20 years we'll still have to sit behind a wheel…"[72]. If you read the popular media and the press releases put out by motor manufacturers and the tech giants, then you would be forgiven for thinking that fully self-driving cars are all ready to go. It's only the luddites in government who are blocking things.

In discussing the reasons why my visually impaired grandma probably won't be able to buy a fully autonomous (Stage 5 autonomy[73]) car in 2019/20, and probably not for a decade or more after that, a really great question to ask yourself is: "Where are all the driverless trains (and boats for that matter)?" Surely going up and down the rails is a massively simpler task than driving on the open road or in city traffic? Actually, there are a few driverless train systems in operation, but only a very tiny proportion of the worlds trains are fully automated.[74] Those that are, are local transport and/or underground systems operating in small well controlled environments rather than intercity type trains travelling around the country[75].

Why aren't most, if not all, trains fully automated? There is not a single or simple answer to this. It's partly the tech, partly to do with economics. Unions and public sentiment play their part as do governments and legislation. Arguably the tech issues are the easy part. It's all the other stuff that makes these things difficult.

The real test of the truly autonomous car is when anyone can go and buy one with no restrictions on who they are or where they can go. Being able to go hands free on the freeway for a few miles or having self-driving taxis operating in the centers of a few major cities, does not really pass the test. In truth, when it comes to fully self-driving cars, the answer is that the technology simply isn't good enough. It's getting there, but it's not there yet. If we return to the moon landing analogy, then self-driving tech is probably at about the equivalent of the low earth orbit stage of development. Good progress has been made but there's still a long way to go.

Don't get me wrong, I'm not saying that you won't be able to buy a fully self-driving car at some point and I think it's going to be great when you can, but it's going to be a while yet. The hype is greater than the actuality. What we are seeing in practice are cars with a steadily increasing number of autonomous features, starting with automatic breaking, self-parking and lane assist, with more complex features appearing all the time. However, to get to fully autonomous anyone, anytime, anywhere driverless transport, there are a whole host of niggly issues that are still being worked upon, and I don't mean the often cited "shopping trolley or child" dilemma. Doing an illegal U-turn when the traffic backs up (we've all done it!), pulling out into oncoming traffic, getting out of the way of the emergency services, overtaking a slow-moving tractor on a single lane road and knowing when you are going to have to drive up on the pavement/sidewalk. These are just a few of the things that regular human drivers have to do on a daily basis all over the world. They don't do these things without reason. Sometimes, you have to mount the pavement or overtake when its technically illegal, otherwise you'll just get stuck with dozens of angry drivers pomping their horns behind you. A hand gesture from a fellow driver lets you know it's safe to pull out, even if it doesn't look that way. And to those who say that these things will all be solved when we remove human drivers from the road – that's just purple unicorn fantasy land. The challenge of getting Americans to give up their right to drive would make revoking the second amendment look like a picnic[76].

Finally, who's to say a self-driving car is a self-driving car? Surely there must be some independent official framework and testing process that the vehicles must pass before a manufacturer can say that its cars are self-driving? If I have to pass a driving test then so should a driverless car. Many governments are working on these things but they are still in their infancy.[77]

OK OK – enough moaning about self-driving cars. Why is this relevant to a book like this anyway? Well, the original focus of this chapter was going to be something along the lines of: "Avoiding the hype and identifying the opportunities." I wanted to write about all the interesting ways in which machine learning and artificial intelligence are changing society at large. This is important because changes in how society operates generates both threats and opportunities. New avenues of commerce open up, and old ways of doing things become a distant memory of repetitive hard work and slow, manual, inefficient processes. No one wants what happened to Kodak and Blockbuster[78] to happen to them. Adapt or die.

However, you have to be aware of the risks, barriers and blockers just as much as the opportunities. There is a reason why they call it the bleeding edge of technology. For every new tech success story there are dozens of failures, but we always give a lot more attention to the successes and push the failures to the back of our minds. A common saying is: "It's a wise man who learns from the mistakes of others." However, when I searched Amazon for books on "Business failure" the number of results returned was less than 5% of the number returned when searching for "Business success."[79]

The different amounts of attention we give to success and failure often translates into an unrealistic expectation of how new technologies will impact us. Self-driving cars are a prime example of this effect. They demonstrate the excessive optimism of Silicon Valley and the over-hyping of new technologies that often occurs. Virtual reality and wearable tech are a couple of other examples that are now a bit further down the line. Massively hyped initially, did not take over the world, but they do have some really useful real-world applications.

In fact, most new technologies traverse this path. The technology often proves useful in the long run, but rarely achieves the highs that the techno-evangelists suggested when the technology was first envisaged. If you want to obtain a general view of this over-hyping effect in practice, then I can't recommend the **Gartner Hype Cycle** highly enough[80]. This principle is also captured by Amara's Law:

"We tend to overestimate the effect of a technology in the short run and underestimate the effect in the long run.[81]"

In 2012, Gartner reported autonomous vehicle technology as being 5-10 years from maturity. Five years later in 2017, this figure had been revised upward to more than 10 years.

Another, more general, example of the hype around AI technologies are the estimates on the number of jobs that will be lost due to AI driven automation over the next couple of decades. Make no mistake, AI is a disruptive technology. Many people will lose their jobs or have to adapt to different ways of working because of it, but it's not going to replace everything that we do – at least not in the next 10-20 years.

The most influential study of its day[82] in 2013, put the number of jobs at high risk of being lost due to automation at 47%. The study estimated that by sometime around 2030-2035[83] almost half of all jobs in the US currently done by people would be done by machines. The estimates for other advanced economies such as the UK and Germany were similar. Over time, this estimate has been revised down. In 2017, PwC suggested an upper limit of 38%[84] A comprehensive study by the OECD was quoting a figure of just 10% by 2018[85], and that's not taking into account all the extra jobs that will be created to support these new technologies. That's still a pretty big impact, but a lot smaller than what was originally being talked about. If you spread those jobs losses over a 20 year period, then that equates to just 1 in 200 jobs lost each year – not taking into account the new jobs that will be created.

Taking all this in the round, the usual rules apply. From a business perspective, AI isn't really any different from any other technological development. You need to assess the impacts and take a view as to if, where and how AI based technologies are going to useful. Don't blindly follow the herd. Just because everyone else says they are doing it does not necessarily mean it's right for you. Of course, you mustn't stick your head in the sand. You should be proactive in seeking out new ideas and different ways of working, but make your own assessment of the value that artificial intelligence and machine learning can add. Also, don't rely on third parties, with an interest in selling you a solution, to quantify the benefits for you.

Almost daily, I get e-mails from data science companies offering to revolutionize my IT systems, automate my processes and enhance my data analytics capability. How do I work out which ones have something to offer me and which ones are just riding on the coat tails of these technologies?

As we've discussed in previous chapters, the technology has to be applicable to real business problems and processes if it's going to add value. A machine learning based solution will only add value if it helps you to achieve at least one of the following:

- **Reduced costs.** It facilitates doing something more efficiently, such as better warehouse and inventory control or optimizing product pricing.

- **Improved quality.** The solution delivers better products and services. For example, faster fulfilment of customer orders or reducing customer complaints.

- **Creates new opportunities.** Machine learning acts as enabler to allow you to do something that you've not been able to do before. Maybe this is to enter new markets or provide different types of products and services.

One thing to look out for is what I term the "data opportunist." I've come across more than one analytics company who have suggested that I just: "Employ a few of our data scientists to see what we can discover from your data." There is no in-depth probing of what I or my organization does, what our problems are or where our inefficiencies lie. It's just assumed that by paying these guys to trawl my data, and maybe churn out a few predictive models, they will deliver something useful.

I remember talking to a friend of mine recently, who had hired some data scientists to do exactly this for his organization (a financial services company). They said they could help him predict which customers were about to cash in their investments. So, this was an attrition type problem – identify customers who are likely to leave and then try to entice them to stay.

My friend told me, that after many weeks of work, the data scientists he had hired delivered a predictive model that essentially predicted retirement; i.e. people approaching retirement tend to review their investments in preparation for giving up work. The data scientists seemed very happy with what they had found. However, this was something that my friend and everyone in the industry already knew. The exercise added no value but cost tens of thousands of dollars to undertake. I could describe a whole host of other similar situations, but I think you get the idea.

Another thing you should do is think about what's going on in your industry and with your competitors. Talk to you network of contacts. See what others are doing in your problem space. If no one else is using artificial intelligence/machine learning technologies for that type of problem then you are in a high risk space. Maybe you can be a trailblazer and can get ahead of the pack by being the first to reap the benefits. Alternatively, maybe you are taking a massive gamble that's unlikely to pay off. If no one else has adopted the technology for that purpose then that's a risk.

If you have a high-risk culture, and taking chances is all part of the game, then go for it. However, if like most of us, you are operating in a more conservative environment and a potential risk of failure is getting the sack, then think carefully before diving in. You need to do your homework and make sure that the benefits that are promised will be delivered. At the very least, when the dust settles many months later, you need to be able to show that your decisions were rational and based on what you knew at the time.

One possible strategy to follow when engaging with suppliers, particularly when the value of a proposition is vague or uncertain, is to suggest a shared return model of contractual engagement. A clearly defined set of objectives are agreed up-front and the supplier takes a cut of the profit (or loss) that results. If a suppler is selling you all the benefits of their machine learning based solutions, but won't entertain a shared risk/reward model of compensation, then ask yourself why that might be? Even if you don't really want to go down this route, the response you get from the supplier will be informative.

Also bear in mind that just because it's possible to automate something doesn't mean that you have to or that it's desirable to do so. Silicon Valley has a reputation for developing innovative gadgets and then trying to find a market for them, rather than starting with people's problems and then trying to find solutions. If we go back to self-driving cars – do we know how many people actually want a self-driving car? The most recent consumer studies suggest that at the moment it's only a minority[86]. That may change in time, but it's something that the motor manufactures should be mindful of.

Overall, what I'm trying to get across in this chapter is keep an open mind, but also a level head. AI and machine learning present massive opportunities to do things better, more efficiently and more cheaply. However, just like any other aspect of business – don't jump in until you know what the opportunities are, you know want you want to do and why, and you've done a proper benefits case to support your decision. Good Luck!

16. Concluding Remarks

First, I would like to thank you for taking the time to purchase and read this concise introduction to the world of artificial intelligence and machine leaning for business. I hope that you now have an understanding of what these things are, why they are important and how they work. Equally importantly, I hope that you understand that while these are essentially mathematically based topics, they can only realize their full potential when relevant business, social, ethical, political and legal issues are taken into consideration.

If you liked the book, then please consider giving it a positive review on Amazon, Goodreads or other review sites. As an independent publisher, this sort of support is very helpful and is much appreciated.

If on the other hand, you felt the book didn't fill the void in your life that you were expecting it too, then I'm very sorry to hear that. Please feel free to drop me a line to let me know why at:

AI@relativistic.co.uk

Likewise, if you have any positive feedback I'll be more than happy to receive that too.

Steven Finlay

21st June 2018

Appendix A. Evaluating Predictive Models

Once a predictive model has been constructed it needs to be assessed to determine how well it predicts behavior. Sometimes there is a single cut-off score that results in the business objective being met, which can be established by looking at the score distribution table (such as those in Figures 3, 4 and 6). Similarly, for things like object recognition systems where each score represents one outcome, you simply choose the outcome with the highest score.

In many situations however, there is not one single cut-off score to choose. Instead, there is a range of possible cut-offs. Any one of these cut-offs will deliver the original business objective, but with different benefits and drawbacks. Likewise, common practice is to build several different predictive models. The performance of the models are then compared against each other so that the best one is chosen.

If you think back to the heart disease case study, used throughout this book, then you will remember that we looked at a decision tree model and a scorecard model. Both models provided solutions that met the stated business objective; i.e. identify at least 50% of people who will develop heart disease but invite no more than 5% of the entire population for a check-up. However, the scorecard model performed better overall. This is because it identified 62% of cases within the highest scoring 5% whereas the decision tree only identified 55%

You could also argue that both models over delivered. They identified more than the required 50% of cases. What this means is that there is actually some flexibility in how the cut-off is chosen; i.e. there is more than one cut-off that meets the objective. In this situation, two possible ways in which the model could be used are:

1. **Maximize outcomes.** Choose the cut-off which results in exactly 5% of the population being invited for a check-up; i.e. use all available resources. This will result in more than 50% of heart disease cases being identified (this is the answer presented previously in the case study; i.e. the 521 cut-off score for the scorecard or the 12 cut-off score for the decision tree).

2. **Minimize resources.** Choose the cut-off which results in exactly 50% of heart disease cases being invited for a check-up. This means that less than 5% of the population will be invited for a check-up because a cut-off score above 521 would be chosen.

Which option to choose depends on what's most important to the health authority. If it wants to maximize the identification of heart disease then option 1 is best. If it wants use as little resources as possible then option 2 is better. The health authority could of course, also choose a cut-off score that lies somewhere between these two extremes.

More generally, in these types of situations there are two considerations when choosing cut-offs:

• **Purity (Lift).** If a high cut-off is chosen, then only a few cases will be selected, but of those selected a high proportion will display the characteristic you are interested in.

• **Volume (Gain).** If a lower cut-off is chosen, then more cases will be selected and overall more cases of interest will be within the selected group (those above the cut-off). However, the purity of selected cases will fall; i.e. a lower proportion of those above the cut-off will display the characteristic you are interested in.

To help decide on cut-off strategies and the trade-off between purity and volume, two popular tools that are used to assess the impact of different cut-off strategies are **Lift Charts** and **Gains Charts**. These provide an easy to use visual representation of how a model performs.

Starting with lift charts, these provide a view of purity. Figure 13 provides an example of a lift chart for the heart disease scorecard that was presented in Figure 2.

Figure 13. A lift chart for the heart disease scorecard.

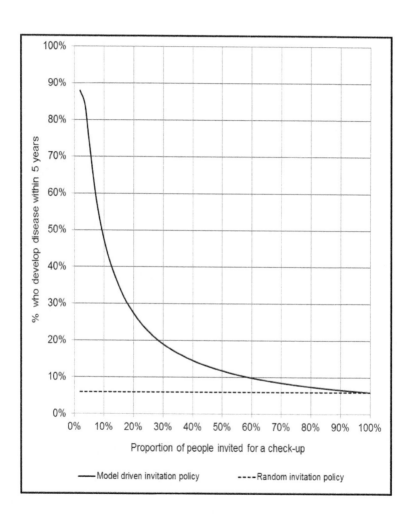

In Figure 13 the X axis shows the proportion of people invited for a check-up. The Y axis shows the proportion of those who are invited who can be expected to develop the disease within 5 years. The dotted straight line is the base rate. The base rate is the percentage of people expected to develop heart disease over the next 5 years within the population at large i.e. 6%. To put it another way, the base rate represents a random selection strategy for inviting people for check-ups.

The solid curved line shows what would happen if the prioritization process for deciding who to invite for a check-up was based on the scores from the scorecard model. For example, the graph shows that if the highest scoring 40% of the population are invited for a check-up then about 15% of these would develop heart disease in the future. If volumes were reduced and say, only 10% were invited for a check-up, then the proportion (purity) would rise to around 50%

The smaller the proportion targeted for medical intervention, the higher the proportion with the disease. To put it another way, if you only target the small number of people in the population with the very highest scores, then one can expect a very high proportion of those selected to have heart disease. If the invited group is enlarged however, by including people with lower scores, then overall the proportion correctly identified (the purity) will fall.

The lift chart is therefore a way of comparing trade-offs between volume and purity.

How has the lift chart been produced? Figure 14 shows an extended version of the score distribution table for the heart disease scorecard that was first introduced in Figure 3.

Figure 14. Extended score distribution table.

Score range From	To	Number of people	% of population	Number with heart disease after 5 yrs.	% with heart disease after 5 yrs.	Descending cumulative				Purity (Lift)
						Number of people	% of population	Number with heart disease after 5 yrs.	% with heart disease after 5 yrs.	
0	300	55,950	11.19%	40	0.07%	500,000	100.00%	30,000	6.00%	6.00%
301	320	56,606	11.32%	68	0.12%	444,050	88.81%	29,960	6.75%	6.75%
321	340	59,700	11.94%	129	0.22%	387,444	77.49%	29,892	7.72%	7.72%
341	360	58,706	11.74%	216	0.37%	327,744	65.55%	29,763	9.08%	9.08%
361	380	64,429	12.89%	403	0.63%	269,038	53.81%	29,547	10.98%	10.98%
381	400	52,749	10.55%	575	1.09%	204,609	40.92%	29,144	14.24%	14.24%
401	420	34,089	6.82%	600	1.76%	151,860	30.37%	28,569	18.81%	18.81%
421	440	21,107	4.22%	632	2.99%	117,771	23.55%	27,969	23.75%	23.75%
441	460	17,269	3.45%	878	5.09%	96,664	19.33%	27,337	28.28%	28.28%
461	480	23,364	4.67%	2,020	8.65%	79,395	15.88%	26,459	33.33%	33.33%
481	500	17,477	3.50%	2,553	14.61%	56,031	11.21%	24,439	43.62%	43.62%
501	520	13,554	2.71%	3,366	24.84%	38,554	7.71%	21,885	56.77%	56.77%
521	540	7,103	1.42%	3,463	48.76%	25,000	5.00%	18,519	74.08%	74.08%
541	560	8,260	1.65%	6,587	79.74%	17,897	3.58%	15,056	84.12%	84.12%
561	999	9,637	1.93%	8,469	87.88%	9,637	1.93%	8,469	87.88%	87.88%
		500,000		30,000	6.0%					

The first four of the extra columns on the right in Figure 14 show descending cumulative figures; i.e. they show the number and proportion of cases scoring at or above a given score. The lift (rightmost column) is calculated by dividing the cumulative number of people with heart disease by the cumulative total. For example, the lift at a score of 501 is calculated as:

$$Lift = 21,885 / 38,554 = 56.77\%$$

This means that 56.77% of those scoring above 501 are expected to develop heart disease. The lift chart is then created by plotting the cumulative % of population column against the lift.

A lift chart provides a purity perspective on the population across the range of possible cut-off scores. A gains chart on the other hand is used to provide a volume orientated view. Figure 15 shows the gains chart for the heart disease scorecard.

The gains chart has been produced by plotting the cumulative percentage of the total population at or above the score, against the cumulative proportion of heart disease cases at or above the same score; i.e. the second and fourth rightmost columns in Figure 14. For example, in Figure 15 it can be seen that if one invites 10% of the population for a check-up, then that will result in about 80% of all heart disease cases in the population being included on the invite list. Similarly, if one invites 30% of the population, then approximately 95% of all cases will be on the invite list.

Figure 15. A Gain chart for the heart disease scorecard.

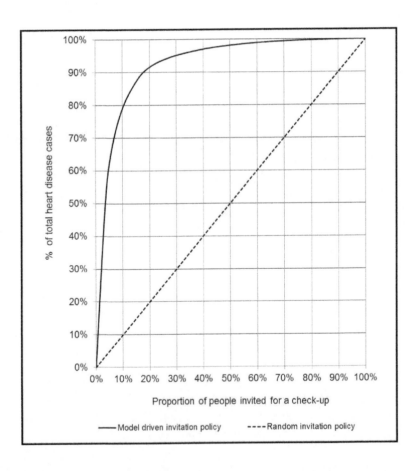

Lift charts and gains charts are very useful tools that can be produced for any type of classification model to help business users decide how models should be used. Similar graphs can also be produced for regression type models.

Data scientists will also use specific metrics to measure how good the overall predictive accuracy of a model is. Perhaps the three most popular measures that are used to do this are:

- **AUC (area under the curve).** This is a popular measure for evaluating classification models. Values of AUC range from 0.5 to 1. A value of 0.5 indicates that a model has no predictive ability; i.e. is useless. A value of 1.0 indicates a perfect predictor that gets it right every time. The often cited GINI statistic and Somers'D are similar measures[87].

- **Percentage correctly classified (PCC).** This is simply the proportion of events that are correctly classified for a given cut-off score. If an event scores above the cut-off score, then the model predicts correctly. If a non-event occurs and it scores below the cut-off then the model has also got it right. For the heart disease scorecard with a cut-off of 521 the proportion of cases correctly classified was 96.4% When people talk about "model accuracy" or the model is "X% accurate" what they are usually referring to is the PCC.

- **(Adjusted) R-squared.** This is the most popular measure for evaluating regression models. It is based on the differences between the actual and predicted values for each observation in the development sample. An R-squared value of zero indicates that a model has no predictive ability; i.e. is useless. A value of 1 indicates a perfect predictor that gets it spot on every time.

Measures such as Adjusted R-squared, AUC and PCC are used to compare the performance of different models and to assess how model performance changes over time. When a new predictive model is built, the performance of the old and new models are compared to see how much better the new model is. Likewise, if two or more different types of model are developed for a given problem, then the one with the highest AUC, PCC, R-Squared and so on will be deemed to be the best; i.e. the most predictive.

There are literally dozens of other metrics that people have developed to measure how well models perform, but AUC and PCC are by far the most popular metrics for assessing the performance of classification models, and Adjusted R-Squared is the most popular measure for assessing regression models.

If you want to learn more about these and other measures for assessing predictive models, then there are a host of online resources available, including a large number of Wikipedia entries.

Appendix B. Further Information and Recommended Reading

The following are some of the primary internet resources for machine learning, artificial intelligence and related technologies (Big data, data mining, etc.)

Operational Database Management Systems. http://www.odbms.org/ This site is supported by a range of industry experts. It covers a wide range of topics relating to the implementation and application of new technologies associated with machine learning, cloud computing and Big Data, amongst other things.

KDnuggets. https://www.kdnuggets.com/ This is one of the leading sites providing resources for data scientists.

AnalyticBridge. http://www.analyticbridge.com/ AnalyticBridge hosts a range of articles, blogs and discussion forums about machine learning that is open to all. There is a broad range of topics covered, from the strategic to the very technical / operational.

LinkedIn. http://www.linkedin.com/ There are several forums on LinkedIn that discuss machine learning and related topics.

Kaggle. https://www.kaggle.com/. Kaggle describes itself as "The home of Data Science and Machine Learning." It provides various resources for data scientists but is perhaps best known for hosting machine learning / AI competitions. Many of these have substantial dollar prizes for the winners. Kaggle competitions are open to anyone. All you need to do is download the data for a given competition and then upload your results. These are automatically assessed within a few seconds and your score is entered onto the competition leader board so that you can see how you rank. A great feature of Kaggle competitions is that you can enter as many times as you like, allowing you to try out lots of different solutions.

StatSoft. http://www.statsoft.com/Textbook. This is a website managed by Dell, providers of the STATISTICA statistical software package. If you want to know more about a wide range of statistical methods, including those used in machine learning, then this is a great site to refer to.

The following is a list of books that are suitable for the general reader; i.e. no formulas or tech speak.

Agrawal, A., Gans, J. and Goldfarb, A. (2018). *Prediction Machines: The Simple Economics of Artificial Intelligence.* **Harvard Business Review Press.** The three authors are economists rather than technical experts. They discuss AI from an economics perspective. In particular, they present the case for AI as a more efficient way to predict those things that are important to business, both strategically and operationally.

Davenport, T. and Kim, J. (2013). *Keeping Up with the Quants: Your Guide to Understanding and Using Analytics.* **Harvard Business Review Press.** Davenport was one of the first people to write an accessible analytics text in his 2006 book – Competing on Analytics. This more recent book is written specifically for non-technical managers to help them understand and work with technically minded people who do machine learning; i.e. data scientists.

Finlay, S. (2014). *Predictive Analytics, Data Mining and Big Data. Myths, Misconceptions and Methods.* **Palgrave Macmillan.** This is one of my books, so I'm bound to say nice things about it. Primarily it's a book about machine learning, but it also provides a brief introduction to Big Data. The main focus is on practical issues around the development and implementation of predictive models.

Information Commissioner's Office (2017). *Big data, artificial intelligence, machine learning and data protection.* **ICO.** This document is a detailed discussion paper produced by the UK government. It examines the implications for Big Data, machine learning and artificial intelligence from a data protection perspective. It provides a very comprehensive view of the issues that need to be considered when dealing with these new technologies, particularly in relation to the General Data Protection Regulation (GDPR) that applies in all EU countries.

Kahneman, D. (2012). *Thinking, Fast and Slow.* **Penguin.** This is a book about decision-making. It digs into the reasons why people make decisions in the way that they do. In particular, it discusses why people often have trouble accepting automated decision-making systems based on machine learning. However, the book is much broader than this. It discusses a wide range of issues associated with human decision-making processes.

O'Neil, C. (2016). *Weapons of Math Destruction. How Big Data Increases Inequality and Threatens Democracy.* **Allen Lane.** This fascinating book presents the "Dark side" of predictive models, discussing the bias and discrimination that can be brought to bear through their use and misuse. Very much complementary to the material in Chapter 13 of this book.

Siegel, E. (2016). *Predictive Analytics: the Power to Predict Who Will Click, Buy, Lie, or Die.* 2nd edition. **Wiley.** Very much a marmite book. You'll either love it or hate it, but it's the book that brought machine learning to the attention of a much wider audience than ever before. I like marmite!

Silver, N. (2012). *The Signal and the Noise: Why So Many Predictions Fail.* **Penguin.** This is not really a machine learning book. However, what is very relevant is the focus on understanding why so many forecasting systems fail. It discusses why more attention needs to focus on the weaknesses and pitfalls of forecasting and prediction, so as to improve the quality of forecasting models in the future.

If you want to tool up and get a bit more into the technical aspects of AI and machine learning, then I recommend the following:

Baesens, B. (2014). *Analytics in a Big Data World: The Essential Guide to Data Science and its Applications.* **Wiley.** This book provides clear descriptions of all the key stages involved in developing a predictive model. A great read for those with a little bit of mathematical and/or statistical knowledge, but you don't need a higher degree in mathematics or statistics to understand the concepts that Baesens puts forward.

Chollet, F. (2018) *Deep Learning with Python.* **Manning Publications.** This well-structured book starts with an introduction as to what artificial intelligence and machine learning are. It then covers off the theory underpinning machine learning before providing coding examples in Python.

Crawley, M. (2012). *The R Book.* **2nd Edition. Wiley.** There are lots of statistical packages that can be used to do machine learning. However, R is one of the most popular. R is open source and can be downloaded for free from the CRAN website http://cran.r-project.org/ If you already have some programming knowledge then this book provides a comprehensive introduction to the R language. Note that the emphasis of the book is on learning R, rather than machine learning.

Easley, D. and Kleinberg, J. (2010). *Networks, Crowds, and Markets: Reasoning About a Highly Connected World.* **Cambridge University Press.** I've not discussed social network analysis in the main part of the text, but social networks are a very important source of data for many types of machine learning models. Companies like Facebook, Google and LinkedIn apply machine learning to the data they hold to drive their advertising and target marketing activities. This book provides a blend of practical and theoretical material about the application of social network analysis in a number of environments.

Goodfellow, I, Bengio, Y. and Courville A. (2016*). Deep Learning (Adaptive Computation and machine learning Series)*. **MIT Press**. At almost 800 pages in length, reviewers have described this as the "Bible" of AI and machine learning. You probably need to be comfortable dealing with mathematics and statistics to get the most out of this book.

Hastie, T., Tibshirani, R. and Friedman, J. (2017). *The Elements of Statistical Learning: Data Mining, Inference, and Prediction.* **(Springer Series in Statistics) 2nd edition. Springer.** A detailed and technical guide to many of the data mining tools used in machine learning, written by three of the world's leading academics in the field.

Hosmer, D. and Lemeshow, S. (2013). *Applied Logistic Regression* **(Wiley Series in Probability and Statistics). 3rd edition Wiley.** Logistic regression remains one of the most popular and widely used methods for generating predictive models. This is the first book I recommend to people who want to know more about this method.

Khun, M. and Johnson, K. (2013). *Applied Predictive Modeling.* **Springer**. Another well-constructed book in a similar vein to Baesens (above). It combines practical advice with the more mathematical aspects of the subject.

Witten, I. H., Frank, E., Hall, M. A. and Pal, C. J. (2016). *Data Mining: Practical Machine Learning Tools and Techniques,* **4th edition (The Morgan Kaufmann Series in Data Management Systems). Morgan Kaufmann.** This is a detailed reference manual for those interested in practical data mining. I found it provided a nice blend of theory and practice, with many good examples.

Zelle, J. (2016). *Python Programming: An Introduction to Computer Science.* **3rd edition. Franklin, Beedle & Associates.** A useful introduction to the Python programming language.

Appendix C. Popular Terms in Machine Learning and AI

Activation function. An equation (mathematical formula) that is used to transform the raw output of a neuron into its final output (score). Activation functions are often used to force the output of neurons to lie in a fixed range. This is usually between 0 and 1, but some activation functions result in outputs with different ranges. Common activation functions are the logistic function, the hyperbolic tangent function and the identify function. See https://en.wikipedia.org/wiki/Activation_function for a more complete list of activation functions and their derivation.

Algorithm. An algorithm is a set of instructions or procedures executed in sequence to solve a particular problem. In machine learning various algorithms are applied to discover patterns in data and to create predictive models.

Artificial Intelligence (AI). The replication of biological (mainly human) analytical and decision-making capabilities. For example, object and speech recognition, predicting peoples' future behavior and the ability to play games such as chess, poker and Go.

Big Data. A very large collection of varied, changeable data, which is difficult to process using a standard PC/Server; i.e. typically terabytes in size or larger. Big Data technologies make use of advanced computer architectures and specialist software to facilitate the rapid processing of these data sets. Machine learning is one of the primary tools used to extract value from Big Data.

Causation. The reasoning behind why something happened; i.e. the cause of something. Not to be confused with correlation.

Classification model. A predictive model that predicts if a given event will or will not occur. For example, the likelihood that two people will hit it off on a date, the probability that someone will buy a certain type of car, or the chance that a person develops diabetes sometime in the next 10 years. The score generated by a classification model is an estimate of the likelihood of the event occurring. Not to be confused with regression model.

Cluster(ing). Clusters are groups that contain people or things with similar traits. For example, people with similar ages and incomes might be in one cluster, those with similar job roles and family sizes in another. Clustering algorithms are one form of unsupervised learning (see below).

Convoluted (neural) network. A type of deep neural network where not all neurons in a layer are connected to all the neurons in the next layer. With fewer weights, the (very considerable) time required to train a network is much reduced. A classic application is object recognition. Imagine you have an image comprising 256 * 256 (65,536) pixels. A traditional neural network would need 65,536 weights for each neuron in the first layer, one for each pixel! By segmenting the image into say, 64 sub-regions each with 32 *32 pixels and only connecting neurons within each sub-region, the number of weights is reduced to just 1,024 per neuron. This works because the most important features in images are usually close together (i.e. in the same or neighboring sub-regions). Pixels at opposite sides of the image are much less important.

Correlation. One variable is correlated with another if a change in that variable occurs in tandem with a change in the other. It is important to appreciate that this does not necessarily mean that one thing is caused by another (causation), although it might be. Stork migration is correlated with births (more children born in the spring when storks migrate), but stork migration does not cause births!

Cut-off score, *see* decision rule.

Data mining. Data mining is the science of finding useful information in data sets that a human being would be unable to identify easily by casting their eye over it. Data mining makes use of a wide range of algorithms and automated procedures taken from various disciplines which include statistics, computing and artificial intelligence/machine learning.

Data science. The name given to the skill/art of being able combine mathematical (machine learning) knowledge with data and IT skills in a pragmatic way, to deliver practical value add machine learning based solutions.

Data scientist. The name given to someone who does data science. Good data scientists focus on delivering useful solutions that work in real world environments. They don't get too hung up on theory. If it works it works!

Decision rule. Predictive models generate scores. Decision rules are then used to decide how people are treated on the basis of the score. Those who score above a given score (the cut-off score) receive one treatment, those scoring below the cut-off another. For example, when assessing people for a medical condition, only those scoring above the cut-off; i.e. those with the highest risk of developing the condition, are offered treatment.

Decision tree. A type of predictive model created using an algorithm that recursively segments a population into smaller and smaller groups. Also known as a Classification and Regression Tree or CART (Because they can be used for both classification and regression.)

Deep learning. Predictive models based on complex neural networks (or related architectures), containing many neurons spread across many layers. Deep leaning is proving successful at complex problems such as object recognition and language translation.

Development sample. The set of data used by the machine learning process to construct a predictive model. Development samples need to contain at least several hundred cases, but usually larger samples are used containing thousands or millions of cases.

Ensemble. A predictive model comprised of several subsidiary models (as few as 3 or sometimes many thousands). All of the subsidiary models predict the same outcome but have been constructed using different methods and/or using different data. This means that the models don't always generate the same predictions. The ensemble combines all of the individual predictions to arrive at a one final prediction. Model ensembles often (but not always) significantly outperform the best individual model.

Feed forward neural network. A neural network in which the connections are all one way, from one layer of neurons to the next. There are no backward or inter-layer connections. Most neural networks are feed forward networks.

Forecast horizon. Many (but not all) predictive models forecast future unknown events or quantities. The forecast horizon is the time frame over which a model predicts. Marketing models typically predict response over a forecast horizon of hours or days. In medicine, forecast horizons of many years are used when predicting survival probabilities for particular medical conditions.

Gains chart. A commonly used visual tool used to demonstrate the benefits of a model. Often used in conjunction with a lift chart. See Appendix A for more information.

Gartner Hype Cycle. The Gartner hype cycle classifies new technologies into five phases which captures the way we tend to over and then under estimate their value, before reaching a level somewhere in the middle. Refer to the Gartner website for more details.https://www.gartner.com/technology/research/methodologies/hype-cycle.jsp

GDPR. General Data Protection Regulation. (Regulation (EU) 2016/679). This regulation applies across all EU countries, replacing and updating previous data protection legislation. The GDPR places several obligations and constraints on how personal data can be gathered, stored and used in EU countries. In the context of this book, a key feature is that it gives people certain rights over how automated decision-making systems are used to make decisions about them (such as those based on predictive models derived using machine learning).

General AI. Artificial systems, which act in a human intelligent way across many different problem domains, and which can adapt to new situations like a human can, are described as possessing general AI. No AI systems in use today can be said to possess general AI. See also Narrow AI.

Hadoop. A data storage solution that makes use of lots of cheap "off the shelf" desktop PCs to store and process massive amounts of data very quickly.

Internet of Things (The). This describes intelligent everyday devices such as fridges, washing machines and even light bulbs which can be connected to the internet or other systems. This enables data about their use to be gathered and for users to be able to control these devices remotely e.g. set the washing machine going when I'm on my way home via a smartphone app.

K-Means Clustering. A popular clustering approach. It aims to group observations in a population into K similar groups, based on minimizing the observed differences between observations in each cluster.

Lift chart. A widely used graphical tool for demonstrating the practical benefits of a predictive model. Often used in conjunction with a Gains chart. See Appendix A for more information.

Linear model. A popular type of predictive model that is easy to understand and use. A score is calculated by multiplying the value of each characteristic by its relevant weight and then summing up all the results. A popular way of representing linear models is in the form of a scorecard, such as the one introduced in Chapter 5.

Linear regression. One of the most popular methods for creating linear models and scorecards. Its development dates back more than 100 years. Linear regression requires orders of magnitude less computing power than advanced methods such neural networks. Therefore, it can be used very successfully as a preliminary data selection/modelling tool, to reduce the size of a data set when methods such as (deep) neural networks are being used for the final model.

Logistic regression. A very simple and popular method used for creating classification models. Logistic regression is widely used to create linear models and scorecards, such as the heart disease scorecard introduced in Chapter 5.

Machine learning. Machine learning is the process of finding features (patterns in data). Machine learning algorithms derive from research into artificial intelligence and pattern recognition. The algorithms used to train (deep) neural networks and support vector machines are two examples of machine learning approaches.

MapReduce. A programming approach which enables data stored on Hadoop (and other Big Data platforms) to be processed very quickly. MapReduce works by splitting data processing tasks into lots of smaller sub-tasks that can then be implemented in parallel across the network of computers that comprise a Hadoop network.

Model. A mathematical representation of a real-world system or situation. The model is used to determine how the real-world system would behave under different conditions. See also predictive model.

Monitoring. The performance of predictive models tends to deteriorate over time. It is therefore prudent to instigate a monitoring regime following model implementation to measure how models are performing on an ongoing basis. Models are redeveloped when the monitoring indicates that a significant deterioration in model performance has occurred.

Narrow AI. Artificial intelligence applications which are very good at just one or two things, but which cannot be applied beyond the problems for which they have been designed. All AI applications in use today can be described as being Narrow AI systems. See also General AI.

Neural network. A popular type of predictive model derived using machine learning. Neural networks are well suited to capturing complex interactions and non-linarites in data in a way that is analogous to human learning. "Deep" neural networks (Deep learning/Deep belief networks) are very large and complex neural networks, often containing thousands or millions of artificial neurons, which are used for "AI" tasks such as speech recognition and navigation systems in self-driving cars.

Neuron. The key component of a neural network, which is often discussed as being analogous to biological neurons in the human brain. In reality, a neuron is a linear model whose score is then subject to a (non-linear) transformation. A neural network can therefore be considered as a set of interconnected linear models and non-linear transformations.

Odds. A way to represent the likelihood of an event occurring. The odds of an event are equal to $(1/p) - 1$ where p is the probability of the event. Likewise, the probability is equal to $(1/Odds+1)$. Odds of 1:1 is the same as a probability of 0.5, odds of 2:1 a probability of 0.33, 3:1 a probability of 0.25 and so on.

Over-fitting. The bane of a data scientist's life. Over-fitting occurs when an algorithm goes too far in its search for correlations in the data used to develop a predictive model. The net result is that the model looks to be very predictive when measured against the development sample but performs very poorly when it's used to predict new outcomes using data that has not been presented to the model before.

Override rule. Sometimes, certain actions must be taken regardless of the prediction generated by a model. For example, a predictive model used to target people with offers for beer might predict that some children are very likely to take up the offer. An override rule is therefore put in place to prevent offers being sent to children, regardless of the score generated by the model.

Predictive analytics (PA). The application of machine learning techniques to generate predictive models. Some would argue that for all practical purposes machine learning and predictive analytics are more or less the same thing, given that they use the same types of data as inputs, apply the same type of algorithms and generate similar outputs (scores).

Predictive model. A predictive model is the key output produced by most machine learning algorithms. The model captures the relationships (correlations) that the process has discovered. Once a predictive model has been created, it can then be applied to new situations to predict future, or otherwise unknown, events.

Predictive modelling, *see* predictive analytics.

Principle Component Analysis (PCA). PCA is a popular variable reduction method. PCA uses the original set of variables to construct a new, smaller set of variables, which are then used in the machine learning process. PCA works on the premise that many variables are correlated with each other to a degree; i.e. contain some of the same information. Therefore, this information can be captured more efficiently using fewer variables.

Profiling. Profiling, as defined by the General Data Protection Regulation (GDPR), is: "any form of automated processing of personal data consisting of the use of personal data to evaluate certain personal aspects relating to a natural person, in particular to analyze or predict aspects concerning that natural person's performance at work, economic situation, health, personal preferences, interests, reliability, behavior, location or movements."[88] Profiling may or may not form part of an automated decision-making process.

Python. Along with R, Python is one of the most popular, freely available, software packages used for machine learning.

R. The R language is one of the most popular software platforms for undertaking machine learning. The R software is free and open source, with the user community able to develop new functionality and share it with other users. For those wanting to become data scientists, then a good grounding in R (and/or Python) is recommended. Some books on R and Python are discussed in Appendix B.

Random forest. Random forests are an ensemble method, based on combining together the outputs of a large number of decision trees. Each decision tree is created under a slightly different set of conditions and hence, generate different scores. Random forests are one of the most successful and widely applied ensemble methods.

Recurrent neural network. A type of neural network that uses the outputs from previous cases in the development sample as inputs for sub-sequent training. These types of network are particularly useful where there are sequential patterns in data; i.e. the ordering of cases in the development sample is important. One example is analysis of video. The changes in state from one images to the next (i.e. as objects move) can provide a lot of information about the nature of the current image.

Regression model. A popular tool for predicting the magnitude of something. For example, how much someone will spend or how long they will live. This is in contrast to a classification model which predicts the likelihood of an event occurring.

Reinforcement learning. The process whereby the weights in a model are refined on a case-by-case basis, based on some measure of the success or reward resulting from an action being taken. Each time the model produces an outcome, the quality of that outcome is assessed. The training algorithm then adjusts the model weights depending on how well it performed. Reinforcement learning is viewed as being more similar to the way people learn than other types of machine learning; i.e. supervised learning.

Response (choice) modeling. This term refers to marketing models used to predict the likelihood that someone buys a product or service that they have been targeted with. A response model is a type of classification model.

Score. Most predictions generated by predictive models are represented in the form of a single number (a score). For a classification model the score is a representation of the probability of an event occurring e.g. how likely someone is to respond to a marketing communication or the probability of them defaulting on a loan. For a regression model the score represents the magnitude of the predicted behavior e.g. how much someone might spend, or how long they might live.

Scorecard. A scorecard is a way of presenting linear models which is easy for non-experts to understand. The main benefit of a scorecard is that it is additive; i.e. a model score is calculated by simply adding up the points that apply. There is no multiplication, division or other more complex arithmetic.

Score distribution. A table or graph showing how the scores from a predictive model are distributed across the population of interest. Lift and Gain charts are both ways of presenting the score distribution in a graphical form.

Sentiment analysis. This is a popular technique for extracting information about peoples' attitude towards things. For example, if they had a positive or negative experience when using a particular product or service. In machine learning, sentiment analysis is used to extract information from text or speech that is then used to build predictive models or derive clusters.

Supervised learning. The application of machine learning where each case in the development sample has an associated outcome which one wants to predict. The cases are said to be "Labeled." An example of supervised learning in target marketing is where each customer's response to marketing activity is known (they either responded or they didn't). The model generated by the algorithm is then optimized so as to predict if customers will respond to marketing or not. In practice, most machine learning approaches are examples of supervised learning.

Support vector machine. An advanced type of non-linear model. Support vector machines have some similarities with neural networks.

TensorFlow. An open source library of machine learning algorithms for use with the Python programming language. TensorFlow was originally developed by Google. A key feature of TensorFlow is that it makes use of the processing capabilities of high end graphics cards to significantly increase the speed at which complex machine learning models (deep neural networks in particular) can be developed.

Training algorithm. The term used to describe iterative machine learning algorithms that are used to determine the structure of predictive models. The term is most widely used in relation to neural network type models. The algorithm repeats a number of times, adjusting the weights in the network so as to optimize the network's performance. The training algorithm terminates after a fixed number of iterations or when no further significant improvements in model performance are obtained.

Unsupervised learning. The application of machine learning to problems where the development sample does not contain outcome data. Cases are said to be "Unlabeled." Unsupervised algorithms typically seek to group cases with similar characteristics (features) together. An example of unsupervised learning is an organization wanting to come up with an ad placement policy for an expensive luxury product, where no information exists about customers' purchasing history. Clustering is applied to group similar customers together based on their age, income, gender etc. The ad placement strategy is then targeted at individuals within clusters where the average income is high, rather than clusters with lower incomes.

Validation sample. An independent data set used to evaluate a predictive model after it has been constructed. The validation sample should be completely separate from the development sample and should not be used during model construction. Using one (or more) validation samples is important because machine learning sometimes over-fits a model to the development sample. This means that if you evaluate a predictive model using the development sample it can appear to be more predictive than it actually is.

Appendix D. A Checklist for Business Success

In this appendix, we are going to focus on the questions that you should answer to ensure that your machine learning projects are successful, and that they maximize the benefits that it can bring to business processes. When I say business processes, I am principally talking about replacing or supplementing decision-making tasks that employees might normally do.

The emphasis is on what I've termed "simple AI" type problems in previous chapters. This is where one might be aiming to use a machine learning approach to do things such as deciding which job applicants to interview, making preliminary diagnosis of medical scans, deciding how customers should be treated and so on. The advice in this section may be less relevant to the development of "complex AI" systems such as the operation of autonomous vehicles or the development of personal digital assistants. However, much of the advice remains valid for these types of application as well.

What follows is a concise list of questions you should ask when considering the use of machine learning within your organization. Or as I like to call it: **"Dr F's checklist for machine learning success."**

Unless you can answer **all** of these questions with a high degree of certainty before the project leaves the business requirements phase, then there is a very real chance that the project will fail. Consequently, you risk ending up spending a lot of time and money on the project with no benefits to show at the end of it.

1. **What is your business problem?** Machine learning has no intrinsic value in itself. It has to be applied to a specific problem or objective if it's going to be of any value. If you can't identify a business problem to address then stop right now!

2. **What metric do you wish to optimize?** This should be something that can be measured in simple terms and which is important to you. Time saved, increased profit, reduced cost, customer satisfaction and lives saved are all typical examples. This is what the machine learning process will be used to optimize.

3. **What type of decision rules and actions will you apply?** You have to make decisions based on what the output from the machine learning process is telling you and then act upon those decisions. If you can't think what you will do with a predictive model then why have it?

4. **Where will the data to do machine learning come from?** Machine learning requires at least several hundred, and ideally many thousands, of example cases to work with. For most machine learning problems, the metric of interest (item 2 above) needs to be available for these cases.

5. **How will you operationalize the machine learning process?** What system or process will the predictive models and decisions rules be implemented within? This will require time and money. Who will do it and who will pay for it? The models and decision rules won't implement themselves.

6. **What are the ethical and legal risks associated with automation?** Use the guidelines in Chapter 13 to assess these based on customer impact, data immutability and beneficiaries. What mitigation will you undertaken to manage any risks? Have you also considered the data protection laws that apply in your region?

7. **Is all required data available operationally?** Make the data scientist provide a checklist against every data item that features in their models. This is to ensure that the data that the models need exists within the implementation platform. If any data items are unavailable then you won't be able to use the solution that's been developed.

8. **Is the solution being implemented in an active or passive way, as described in Chapter 11?** If it's in a passive way, what controls do you need to ensure that overriding only occurs when it's right to do so? If people review, and potentially override, every decision made by the system, then the system will not add any value.

9. **How will you assess the success of the project?** The theoretical benefits presented at the end of the analytical phase of a machine learning project are only indicative of what actually happens in real life. A monitoring process is needed to assess the system when it goes live. This is so that you can measure the actual benefits that are realized against those that were promised.

10. **What are the ongoing costs of maintaining the system?** Over time, new data, new regulations, changing business requirements and so on, will mean that the system will require modification and may eventually need to be redeveloped from scratch. How often is this expected to occur and how much is it likely to cost? Don't forget to include costs for regulatory compliance and annual audits.

My advice to you if you are new to machine learning, is to take this list with you whenever you go and meet suppliers of AI/machine learning solutions. In addition to answering these questions for yourself, how the supplier responds to them will give you a good indication of their understanding of your requirements. If they can only answer in terms of general benefits or vague statements about needing to keep up with the competition, then beware.

About the Author

Steven Finlay is a data scientist with more than 20 years' experience of developing practical "value add" machine learning solutions in large scale data environments. He holds a PhD in predictive modelling and is an honorary research fellow at Lancaster University in the UK.

Steve has previously been employed by one of the UK's top 10 banks to manage their suite of credit risk models, has developed machine learning approaches for the UK government and worked for a number of consultancy groups. He is currently Head of Analytics for Computershare Loan Services (CLS) in the UK.

Dr Finlay has published a number of practically focused books about machine learning, artificial intelligence and financial services. His other books (published by Palgrave Macmillan) include:

- Predictive Analytics, Data Mining and Big Data. Myths, Misconceptions and Methods.

- Credit Scoring, Response Modeling and Insurance Rating. A Practical Guide to Forecasting Consumer Behavior.

- The Management of Consumer Credit. Theory and Practice.

- Consumer Credit Fundamentals.

Notes

1 Predicting consumer behavior is a very common application of machine learning, but there many are others. For example, the same techniques are used to predict stock prices, when complex machines are likely to break down and which organizations are likely to become bankrupt.

2 The original role of credit reference agencies (also known as credit reporting agencies or credit bureaus) was as a central repository for data about debts and loan repayments. This is still at the core of what they do, but these days credit reference agencies also hold all sorts of other personal information. Consequently, a credit report can contain a wide variety of personal data in addition to information about a person's credit history. Credit reference agencies were arguably the first "Big Data" companies, decades before the term began to be applied to the likes of Google, Amazon, Facebook, et al.

3 Siegel, E. (2016). 'Predictive Analytics: The Power to Predict Who Will Click, Buy, Lie, or Die.' 2nd Edition. Wiley.

4 See, for example, the arguments made by Roger Penrose in his books: 'The Emperor's New Mind: Concerning Computers, Minds, and the Laws of Physics' and 'Shadows Of The Mind: A Search for the Missing Science of Consciousness.'

5 Cellan-Jones, R. (2017). 'Can Google police YouTube?' BBC http://www.bbc.co.uk/news/technology-39338009, accessed 12/05/2018.

6 Kelion, L. (2018). 'YouTube toughens advert payment rules'. BBC http://www.bbc.co.uk/news/technology-42716393, accessed 12/05/2018.

7 The first applied research into predicting individual consumer behavior was by David Durand. Durand, D. (1941). 'Risk Elements in Consumer Instalment Financing' 1st edition. New York: National Bureau of Economic Research. This was based on work by the famous statistician R.A Fisher. Fisher, R. A. (1936). 'The use of multiple measurements in taxonomic problems.' Annals of Eugenics. 7 (2): pp 179–188.

8 Least squares and related methods were developed in the early part of the

20th century and logistic regression in the 1960s. Neural networks and decision trees came to prominence in the 1980s and ensemble methods, such as random forests, bagging and gradient descent, were invented in the 1990s. Most recent advances in machine learning, such as "deep reinforcement learning" represent an evolution rather than a revolution of these existing methods.

9 Microsoft Azure. https://azure.microsoft.com/en-gb/services/machine-learning/?&wt.mc_id=AID529440_SEM

10 Google Cloud Prediction API. https://cloud.google.com/prediction/

11 Alexa Voice Service (AVS) https://developer.amazon.com/public/solutions/alexa/alexa-voice-service/getting-started-with-the-alexa-voice-service accessed 05/04/2018.

12 https://www.kaggle.com/

13 At the time of writing, the largest prize offered was the Zillow prize for a real estate valuation model. This had a prize fund of £1.2m dollars. https://www.kaggle.com/c/zillow-prize-1. Accessed 03/02/2018.

14 Many, but not all credit scores are scaled in this way. More formally, the "standard" scaling for credit scoring models is for a score of 500 to equate to a 50% chance of being a good payer (odds of 1:1). The odds then double every 20 points. A score of 520 means 2:1 odds of being a good repayer (66% chance of repaying the loan) , a score of 540 odds of 4:1 (80% chance of repaying the loan) and so on.

15 O'Neil, C. (2016). 'Weapons of Math Destruction.' Alan Lane.

16 Lee, D. (2016) 'Tay: Microsoft issues apology over racist chatbot fiasco.' BBC http://www.bbc.co.uk/news/technology-35902104. Accessed 06/04/2018.

17 There are lots of different types of heart disease with different causes and symptoms, but for the sake of simplicity we'll consider heart disease as a single condition for this example.

18 Body Mass Index (BMI) is calculated as a person's weight in kilograms divided by their height in metres squared. For someone who is 180cm tall and weighs 80kg their body mass index is: $80/(1.8 * 1.8) = 24.69$. In the UK, a BMI of 19-25 is considered normal. A BMI under 19 indicates a person may be underweight. 25-30 indicates that someone is likely to be overweight and more than 30 obese. Note that BMI is only a guide, and other factors such as build, age and muscle mass are also important. Some athletes would be classified as overweight using BMI due to having more than the average amount of muscle mass.

19 There are lots of algorithms that can be applied to generate scorecards, but the most popular method is called "Logistic regression." Other popular approaches include genetic algorithms, linear programming and discriminant analysis (linear regression).

20 In practice, a single combined sample would be created initially. This would then be split randomly into two parts (development and validation

samples) before any machine learning was applied. In this example the development and validation samples have been split 50/50 with the same number of cases in each sample, but this need not be the case. Common practice is to assign perhaps 70% or 80% of cases to the development sample and only 30% or 20% to the validation sample. In this way, more data is available for developing the model which should lead to a better, more predictive model.

21 Using a new sample of data to evaluate a predictive model is important when evaluating how good the model is. This is because when predictive models are constructed a major concern is a problem called **Over-fitting**. Over-fitting means that the machine learning process has been over-optimistic. It finds relationships in the development sample that don't exist in the wider population. Consequently, when a predictive model is being evaluated it's always wise to use a validation sample to measure the model's performance. The validation sample should be a completely independent sample that was not used to construct the model.

22 The minimum possible score for this model is 281. The maximum possible score is 605.

23 Calculated as: 1 / 0.0176.

24 Note that this is an artificial example and not a genuine model developed for use by health practitioners. Therefore, you should not take the predictions generated by the model to be a true representation of your (or anyone else's) chance of developing heart disease.

25 In practice, several validation samples would be taken rather than just one. At least one of these would be an "out of time" sample, from a different time period to the development sample. If the results from the various validation samples tell a similar tale, then that is usually sufficient to indicate that the model will work as intended; i.e. that its predictive performance and accuracy will be similar to that observed from the validation / out of time samples.

26 Best is usually determined by an appropriate statistical measure that considers both the incidence (purity) and proportion (number) of cases in each partition.

27 This is generally true, but not universally true. There are occasionally problems where one particular type of model or algorithm is significantly better/worse than another. Generally, its good practice to build a few different types of model to see if this is the case or not.

28 Rosenblatt, F. (1958). 'The perceptron: A probabilistic model for information storage and organisation in the brain'. Psychological Review 65.

29 Their full title is Artificial Neural Network or ANN, but these days, most people just use the term Neural Network.

30 Rumelhart, D. E., Hinton, G. E. and Williams, R. J. (1986). 'Learning representations by back-propagating errors'. Nature 323(6088).

31 i.e. the output from a single neuron (and also a neural network with no second layer) is equivalent to logistic regression, which is a popular statistical method used in machine learning for finding the points associated with a scorecard.

32 This assumes a network with 74 neurons in the first layer and one neuron in the second (output) layer. In the first layer, each of the 74 neurons has one weight for each of the 100 input variables (7,400 weights). The neuron in the output layer has 74 weights, one for each of the outputs from the first layer of neurons. Hence 7,474 weights in total.

33 This is because standard neural networks, where all the inputs are provided to every neuron in the first layer, do not account for the spatial nature of images. For example, the pixels at the top left of an image often have no relation to the pixels at the bottom right. Therefore, it makes sense not to provide all inputs to every neuron.

34 Google Research Blog (2016). 'AlphaGo: Mastering the ancient game of Go with machine learning.' https://research.googleblog.com/2016/01/alphago-mastering-ancient-game-of-go.html. Accessed 06/04/2018.

35 There are also forms of supervised clustering. One such example is the popular K-nearest neighbour approach. When a prediction is required for a new case, the algorithm finds the K cases in the development sample that are most similar to it. The model score is calculated as the proportion of the K cases which displayed the behavior (outcome). If K=200, then the algorithm would find the 200 cases most similar to the case a prediction is required for. If say, 18 out of the 200 cases display the behavior, then the score is 0.09 (18/200). What value of K to use is usually determined by trial and error.

36 There are analytical tools that can collapse a large number of data items into a 2 or 3-dimensional representation, which captures the most important features of those data items. Examples of these methods include principle component analysis and Self-Organizing Maps (SOMs).

37 Experian's Mosaic classifications also exist in US, Germany and many other countries. A host of other companies offer similar clustering based customer profiling products.

38 Typically, this would be achieved by subtracting the mean value of the variable and then dividing by the standard deviation.

39 http://www.experian.co.uk/blogs/latest-thinking/consumer-segmentation-new-data-means-new-insight/ accessed 18/03/2018.

40 It's very difficult to decide up front what the right number of clusters should be. Therefore, trial and error is usually applied. The clustering algorithm is run several times with difference values of K. For each value of K the properties of the resulting clusters are examined, and if deemed to be sufficiently interesting (the clusters have noticeably different features) then that's the value of K to use. If there too many clusters, then some of

the clusters tend to be very similar. If there are too few clusters, then the solution may provide insufficient granularity.

41 The cluster center is calculated as the point where the sum of distances between that point and all of the cases in the cluster is a small as it can be.

42 https://zbmath.org/about/

43 869,666 papers were added to the medline database in 2016. https://www.nlm.nih.gov/bsd/stats/cit_added.html Accessed 04/04/2018.

44 In chess, a standard value assigned to a pawn is 1, a bishop 3, a rook (castle) 5 and so on. Therefore, a simple view of the game can be determined by summing up the value of each players pieces remaining on the board. An actual assessment of who is winning during a game is of course far more complex than this. All advanced chess programs consider the position of the pieces as being just as important, if not more so. However, a simple points based measure of success is very easy to understand and calculate.

45 Knapton, S. and Watson, L. (2017). 'Entire human chess knowledge learned and surpassed by DeepMind's AlphaZero in four hours.' The Telegraph. https://www.telegraph.co.uk/science/2017/12/06/entire-human-chess-knowledge-learned-surpassed-deepminds-alphazero/ Accessed 09/04/2018.

46 Actually, you can – if you use a flight simulator rather than a real plane. This type of approach is one that a number of organizations are pursuing in their developing of autonomous vehicles.

47 If they are included in the machine learning process then the accuracy of the model will be seen to improve in terms of overall accuracy, but that will not be representative of the accuracy of the model as measured on the rest of the population.

48 A naïve way to sample is just to randomly take say, 1 in 10 or 1 in 100 of all cases. A much better approach is to apply stratified sampling. One takes a large proportion of the cases of most interest, and a far smaller proportion of less important cases. If you are trying to predict who repays or defaults on a mortgage, then the most relevant cases are those that default and typically there are not many of these – they are rare events. Therefore, you would sample all of the default cases but only a small proportion of the non-defaults.

49 Standard deviation would be the obvious choice.

50 One "school boy" type error that might have caused this is predicting the inverse of what was intended; i.e. the model scores represent the probability of people repaying their mortgages, not the probability of them defaulting. When the model predicts that default probability is very low, say 0.001% then actually it's the opposite – the probability is 99.999%!!!

51 The conversion of the customers' speech into a numeric format would itself be undertaken using a machine learning derived model. This

preliminary model would identify what words are spoken and replace the actual words with a numeric reference. These numeric references are what would then be used to create various data items that feed the decision-making model under discussion.

52 1 in 5 is actually the marginal error rate. In practice, the error rate will be lower than this because some of the calls will be answered where the probability is between 80 and 100%

53 For example, the individual in question had moved overseas and was therefore beyond the reach of the tax authorities. Likewise, the system often identified people who had become bankrupt. Even though these people technically owe a lot of tax, the tax is uncollectable due to the bankruptcy which has resulted in the person's debts being written off by the courts.

54 The exception to this is where a predictive model is being constructed as a proof of concept. For example, a data scientist may be employed to see if building a predictive model is feasible and would do some experimental model building to see if the project is viable. After all, the last thing you would want to do is build a full end-to-end IT and decision-making infrastructure for machine learning, and then find out that you can't use it.

55 In situations like this, it would probably be possible to derive some type of mapping between net and gross income. However, gross and net income are not always well correlated and depend to some extent on previous tax history, family situation and sources of income.

56 In a strict sense, Big Data covers more than just data about people. The term is also applied to very large amounts of data about processes or systems, such as climate change data, satellite imaging data, traffic data, the data generated by a manufacturing plant and so on.

57 Of course, that is not how it was. Life was just as hard, but the problems were different. Huge amounts of time were spent trying to find clever solutions to maximize limited storage and optimize the very limited processing power available at that time. The software available for machine learning was also far less sophisticated than what is available today.

58 Machine learning requires data to be in numeric or categorical format. Therefore, a key data processing task is to transform all of the data in to this format. For example, creating yes/no indicators to represent positive or negative sentiments expressed in a piece of text, or counters to record the number of times certain words or phrases appear.

59 For example, see the following meta-study: Orlitzky, M., Schmidt, F. L., Rynes, S. L. (2003). 'Corporate Social and Financial Performance: A Meta-analysis.' Organization Studies, volume 24, number 3, pp 403-441.

60 This is similar to the "litmus test" as described by the Information Comissioners Office (ICO) in the UK. ICO (2017). 'Big data, artificial intelligence, machine learning and data protection. V2.2.' pp.78. ICO.

61 Information Commissioners Office. https://ico.org.uk/for-organisations/guide-to-the-general-data-protection-regulation-

gdpr/individual-rights/rights-related-to-automated-decision-making-including-profiling/ Accessed 06/05/2018.

62 GDPR Article 22.

63 GDPR Article 22 gives individual EU governments the ability to define further exceptions. For example, automated decision-making for the purposes of detecting tax evasion or other types of fraud.

64 Council of Europe (2016). CONVENTION FOR THE PROTECTION OF INDIVIDUALS WITH REGARD TO AUTOMATIC PROCESSING OF PERSONAL DATA [ETS No. 108.]. Draft Explanatory Report. Para 75.

65 GDPR recitals 58 and 60.

66 Data Protection Working Party (2017). 'Guidelines on Automated individual decision-making and Profiling for the purposes of Regulation 2016/679'. pp 11.

67 One would probably need to also support this statement by calculating the individual's score assuming that there had been no missed payments and confirming, that in that situation, the application would have been accepted. If the applicant would also have been declined even if there were no missed payments, then additional reasons for the decision would need to be provided.

68 Data Protection Working Party. (2017). 'Guidelines on Automated individual decision-making and Profiling for the purposes of Regulation 2016/679'. pp 14.

69 Information Commissioner's Office (2017). 'Big data, artificial intelligence, machine learning and data protection.' ICO.

70 As required by banks and other deposit taking institutions which calculate their capital reserves using the Internal Rating Based (IRB) approach.

71 BBC (2011). 'IBM's Watson supercomputer crowned Jeopardy king.' BBC http://www.bbc.co.uk/news/technology-12491688 Accessed 06/04/2018.

72 Marks, P. (2012) 'Driverless cars ready to hit our roads.' New Scientist. https://www.newscientist.com/article/mg21328585-300-driverless-cars-ready-to-hit-our-roads/ Accessed 28/03/2018.

73 The industry classifies self-driving technology into 5 Levels. Level 1 covers simple drive assist facilities such as assisted parking and adaptive cruise control. Level 5 is where, in theory, you don't need a steering wheel or other controls – the car can do everything itself.

74 These are trains which can operate automatically all the time, including doing things like detecting obstacles on the tracks and dealing with other types of emergency.

75 Brooks, R. (2017). 'The Big Problem With Self-Driving Cars Is People.' IEEE Spectrum https://spectrum.ieee.org/transportation/self-driving/the-big-problem-with-selfdriving-cars-is-people Accessed

06/05/2018.

76 This is the part of the American constitution that gives citizens the right to bear arms (guns, and plenty of 'em). Anything that comes close to suggesting restrictions on this right (gun control) is a political hot potato.

77 Warren, T. (2018). 'Despite CES hype, self-driving cars are not for sale.' The Verge https://www.theverge.com/2018/1/13/16887728/detroit-auto-show-2018-ces-self-driving-cars-toyota-ford-hype Accessed 06/05/2018.

78 Kodak were the original inventors of the digital camera, but decided not to develop the technology initially. This was because they saw it as a threat to their traditional film based camera business. Their delay in embracing new technology was probably a key feature of Kodak's rapid decline from being one of the world's most recognised brands to bankruptcy in less than a decade. Likewise, Blockbuster where the leading video rental company in the world in the early 2000s, but failed to adapt quickly enough to the rise of online streaming services.

79 I also tried "Management success" and Management failure" as well as just "Failure" and "Success". I got similar results each time.

80 https://www.gartner.com/technology/research/methodologies/hype-cycle.jsp Accessed 06/04/2018.

81 Roy Charles Amara (1925 – 2007) was an American futurologist.

82 Frey, C. and Osborne, M. (2013). 'THE FUTURE OF EMPLOYMENT: HOW SUSCEPTIBLE ARE JOBS TO COMPUTERISATION' Technological Forecasting and Social Change 114.

83 The paper does not give a definitive date but states: "According to our estimate, 47 percent of total US employment is in the high risk category, meaning that associated occupations are potentially automatable over some unspecified number of years, perhaps a decade or two." Which gets us to somewhere around 2030-2035.

84 PwC (2017) 'Up to 30% of existing UK jobs could be impacted by automation by early 2030s, but this should be offset by job gains elsewhere in economy' https://www.pwc.co.uk/press-room/press-releases/Up-to-30-percent-of-existing-UK-jobs-could-be-impacted-by-automation-by-early-2030s-but-this-should-be-offset-by-job-gains-elsewhere-in-economy.html Accessed 06/05/2018. The study made clear that the 38% figure for the US was a theoretical maximum based only on technological feasibility. It did not take into account legal, economic and social issues; i.e. just because it was technically feasible to automate a job did not mean that it would be.

85 Nedelkoska, L. and G. Quintini (2018), 'Automation, skills use and training', OECD Social, Employment and Migration Working Papers, No. 202, OECD Publishing, Paris, http://dx.doi.org/10.1787/2e2f4eea-en. Accessed 06/05/2018.

86 Abraham, H., Reimer, B., Seppelt, B. Fitzgerald, C., Mehler, B. and Coughlin, J. F. (2017) 'Consumer Interest in Automation: Preliminary. Observations Exploring a Year's Change'. MIT working paper 2017-02

87 In theory, there are cases where the AUC can be less than 0.5. However, in practice, that tends to indicate some underlying problem with the way the model has been built, rather than a true representation of the model's performance.

88 GDPR Article 4.

Printed by Amazon Italia Logistica S.r.l.
Torrazza Piemonte (TO), Italy

12970896R00113